England, Scotland, Wales: Unity — God's Gift

JOHN PAUL II

Compiled and Indexed
by the Daughters of St. Paul

ST. PAUL EDITIONS

Reprinted with permission from *L'Osservatore Romano*, English Edition.

A. Mari—cover, 39, 99
Wide World Photos—27, 32, 47, 51, 61, 68,
    89, 106, 131, 168, 176

Library of Congress Cataloging in Publication Data

John Paul II, Pope, 1920-
    England: unity, God's gift.

    Includes index.
    1. Catholic Church—Doctrinal works
—Catholic authors—Addresses, essays, lectures.
2. Catholic Church—Sermons. 3. Sermons, English.
4. Popes—Voyages and travels—Great Britain. I. Title.
BX1755.J643   1983   252'.02   83-8874

ISBN 0-8198-2306-6 cloth
       0-8198-2307-4 paper

Copyright © 1983, by the Daughters of St. Paul

Printed in the U.S.A. by the Daughters of St. Paul
50 St. Paul's Ave., Boston, MA 02130

The Daughters of St. Paul are an international congregation of religious women serving the Church with the communications media.

CONTENTS

Confirmation of the Pastoral Visit
    to Great Britain 11
    During the general audience on May 26, 1982.

Urgent Need Now of Reconciliation 18
    At the London airport at Gatwick, May 28.

I Come at the Service of Unity in Love 20
    *Homily during the concelebrated Mass in
    Westminster Cathedral, May 28.*

The Value of Suffering 28
    *Discourse during a para-liturgical ceremony
    for the sick in Southwark Cathedral, May 28.*

Collaborating for the Good of the
    Universal Church 33
    *To the bishops of England and Wales at the
    residence of Cardinal Hume, May 28.*

The Secular City Has Need of Your Witness 40
    *To the religious men and women of England
    and Wales at the Digby Stuart Training College
    in London, May 29.*

The Richness of What We Share 48
    *Archbishop Runcie's address to Pope John Paul
    at the beginning of the ecumenical service in
    Canterbury Cathedral, May 29.*

Pray and Work for Reconciliation and Unity 52
Address given during the ecumenical ceremony in Canterbury Cathedral, May 29.

Hopes for Growth of Christians
into Deeper Communion 59
To the heads of other Christian Churches and members of the British Council of Churches, May 29.

A People That Does the Will
of the Heavenly Father 62
Homily during a concelebrated Mass in the stadium at Wembly, May 29.

Common Declaration of John Paul II
and the Archbishop of Canterbury 69
Text of the Common Declaration of John Paul II and Archbishop Runcie, read in Canterbury Cathedral, May 29.

Modern Warfare—Totally Unacceptable 73
To a large crowd at Bagington Airport in Coventry, May 30.

May the Generosity of Your Hearts
Never Weaken 80
Reply of Pope John Paul to Archbishop Worlock's address of welcome at Speke Airport in Liverpool, May 30.

The Church Continues Christ's Work
of Reconciliation 84
Homily during the concelebrated Mass in the Metropolitan Cathedral of Christ the King in Liverpool, May 30.

Historical Witness of Polish Emigration 90
To a large group of Polish emigrants in the Crystal Palace Sports Center of London, May 30.

In the Spirit of Vatican Council II 100
To representatives of the Jewish community of England, in the convent of the Sisters of Nazareth in Heaton Park, Manchester, May 31.

Be Ambassadors of Christ and Win Back
the World for God! 101
Homily during a concelebrated Mass in Heaton Park, Manchester, May 31.

Love in the Family Is a Guarantee
for the Future of Humanity 107
Homily during a Mass in Northeast England, May 31.

Let Your Lives Be Formed by the Holy Spirit 114
To the young people of Scotland at Murrayfield Stadium in Edinburgh, May 31.

Love for Our Sacred Calling 121
To the priests and religious of Scotland in Edinburgh Cathedral, May 31.

May Our Desire for Unity Be Hope
for a Divided World 129
To representatives of other Christian Churches in Scotland, at the Archbishop's residence in Edinburgh, June 1.

Assisting the Handicapped—
a Sign of Communion 132
To the handicapped children and their assistants at St. Joseph's Hospital of Rosewell, June 1.

The Cause of Catholic Education 136
To a large group of teachers and students in St. Andrew's College, Glasgow, June 1.

Be Faithful! 146
Homily during a concelebrated Mass in Bellahouston Park, Glasgow, June 1.

Fidelity and Friendship with Christ 158
  To the bishops of Scotland in the Archbishop's residence in Edinburgh, June 1.

Christ Is the True Bread Giving Life
  to the World 162
  Homily during a Mass in Pontcanna Fields in Cardiff, Wales, June 2.

Unity Is God's Gracious Gift 169
  To various Christian communities of Wales in Cardiff Castle, June 2.

I Came to Great Britain
  To Invite You To Pray 170
  To the youth of Wales and England at Ninian Park in Cardiff, June 2.

Great Blessing of Mutual Understanding
  and Respect 175
  Reply of Pope John Paul to the address of the Archbishop of Westminster, June 2.

All Peoples Are United in the Body of Christ 177
  Reflections of the Holy Father upon his return from his pastoral journey to Great Britain, June 9.

Confirmation of the Pastoral Visit to Great Britain

At the general audience on Wednesday, May 26, 1982, Pope John Paul II announced that he would proceed with his planned pastoral visit to Great Britain. He also read the text of a letter he sent to the Church in Argentina explaining his reasons for the decision. The following is the complete text of the Pope's talk.

First of all, I address to you my cordial greeting, and I welcome you with affection to this general audience being held between the Ascension and Pentecost. The liturgy of these days reminds us of the words with which Jesus, comforting His Apostles whom He was about to leave, promised: "When the Counselor comes, whom I shall send to you from the Father, the Spirit of truth who proceeds from the Father, he will bear witness to me; and you also will bear witness to me" (Jn. 15:26).

Beloved, if the duty to bear witness to Christ touches upon every one of the faithful, it binds particularly the successors of the Apostles, who are the bishops, and among them, the Roman Pontiff who, in his capacity as the Successor of Peter, has a direct responsibility with regard to the whole Church. Moved by this awareness, in recent years I have made myself a pilgrim throughout the world, in order to bring to various portions of Christ's flock support in their trials and encouragement to persevere in courageous adherence to the permanent values of the Gospel.

AFTER CONSULTATION

In line with this program, a pastoral visit to the Churches in England, Scotland and Wales has been scheduled and prepared for a long time, as you know. The recent sorrowful events of the conflict in the South Atlantic have cast doubts on carrying out this journey, which so many Christians, not only Catholics but also those of other confessions, are anxiously awaiting. After thorough consultations with the major authorities of those Churches, I have decided to carry out this visit all the same, though making some modifications.

Since, however, this decision could create some surprise or perplexity among the Catholics of the Argentine Church, certainly no less dear and no less close to my heart, I felt the need to explain to them the reasons that led me to this decision after prolonged and difficult reflection.

For this reason I addressed to the sons and daughters of that beloved nation a letter, which I will now read to you.

Beloved sons and daughters of Argentina,

1. I am writing to you in my own hand, because I feel that I must repeat the fatherly gesture of the Apostle Paul towards his children in order to strengthen them in the Faith (cf. Col. 4:18).

I am writing you this letter, moved by a feeling of affection and solidarity toward the one universal

Church, which is found on the whole earth, in all peoples and nations. I am writing to you because I think a special clarification is necessary for you who are living on Argentine soil. This clarification is required by the problems raised by my apostolic and pastoral journey to England, Scotland and Wales during the days of Pentecost of this year.

If in recent weeks there had not taken place the tragic events that are centralized in the southern region of the Atlantic Ocean and are connected with the conflict between your country and Great Britain, this journey would need no explanation, just as no explanation has been necessary for any other journey undertaken to visit the Churches that are in various countries and continents. But doubtlessly, with regard to the present sad circumstances, I am bound to give you this explanation, knowing that you will accept it as loyal testimony of affection in my evangelical service to the world.

SCHEDULED TWO YEARS AGO

2. The Pope's journey to visit the Churches in England, Scotland and Wales had already been scheduled two years ago, and for a year and a half intense preparation has been carried on, taking concrete form in a series of activities of a pastoral nature. The anticipation created for achieving the objective of these preparations is such that I cannot do less than carry out this visit, which happens to crown centuries of fidelity of those Catholics to the Church and to the Pope. On the other hand, despite the insistences I have made to try to postpone my journey, the bishops

of Great Britain have shown, and continue to show, that they are unanimous in maintaining the absolute impossibility of such a delay, which in their judgment would be practically equivalent to a cancellation.

The cancellation of the journey would be a disappointment not only for the Catholics, but also for very many non-Catholics, who consider it, as it truly is, particularly important also for its ecumenical significance. Really, they well know that the Pope's visit has a strictly pastoral character and is in no way political.

This strictly pastoral and ecumenical character is so essential and prevalent that, given the circumstances, the representatives of Her Majesty's government have spontaneously withdrawn from all the contacts that were previously scheduled and which normally have had their place in other circumstances during similar visits.

The program provides for a meeting with the high representatives of the Anglican Communion and with those of the other Christian communities separated from the Catholic Church.

There is, besides, a visit scheduled with Queen Elizabeth, who, as you well know, also holds a very special position within the Church of England.

PRAYING FOR PEACE

3. In undertaking the journey, notwithstanding all the difficulties that are accumulating, and with a soul full of sorrow for the victims of the conflict between Argentina and Great Britain, I nourish the firm hope that gradually an honorable solution through the paths of a peaceful negotiation can soon

be found. For my part, I have not ceased, from the very beginning, working with all the means at my disposal to promote a solution that, while maintaining the character of a decision that is just and adequate for the sense of national honor, would be able to spare both parties, and perhaps also other societies, bloodshed and other terrible effects caused by war. I have prayed many times for this intention, especially during my recent pilgrimage to Fatima, and in a most special way in the Mass celebrated by me on the 22nd of this month in St. Peter's Basilica with the pastors of the Church in Argentina, in Latin America, and those of the Church in England, Scotland and Wales. Still alive in my heart, with all their urgency, are the phrases I spoke on that historic occasion: peace is possible; peace is a pressing duty.

The days of my stay in Great Britain will continue to be an incessant prayer for peace, raised together with the People of God, who bear engraved in their hearts the words of Christ: "Blessed are the peacemakers, for they shall be called children of God" (Mt. 5:9).

TO VISIT ARGENTINA

4. Above all, during these days my thought and my affection will also be with you, beloved sons and daughters of Argentina. My special love for your nation and for all of Latin America, where I have already made two visits, which I keep alive in my heart as universal Shepherd, is well known. In my plans there is also that of paying a third visit at the beginning of next year. Despite this, deeply worried about the cause of peace and moved by love for you, so tried in these moments of sorrow, it would be my

wish even to come directly from England to Argentina, and there, among you and with you, dear brothers and sisters, to raise the same prayer for the victory of a just peace over war. I hope that soon you will be able to join the Pope in the sanctuary dedicated to the Mother of God in Lujan, consecrating your families and your Catholic country to the motherly heart of the Mother of God. This brief journey will not involve giving up a pastoral visit to you, to be made in due time, with an adequate program of its own and with the due preparation.

The Church, while maintaining love toward every single nation, cannot do less than safeguard universal unity, peace and mutual understanding. In this way, also among political tensions and calamities that bring war with them, the Church does not neglect to give witness of the unity of the great human family and to seek ways to emphasize this unity beyond every tragic division. They are the ways that lead to justice, love and peace.

In proof of my affectionate closeness, assuring you of my prayers, I send you a special apostolic blessing.

This is the text of the letter which a representative of mine has brought personally to Argentina.

I ask all of you to join me in prayer to obtain from the Lord, through the intercession of the most holy Virgin, that the purposes of the pastoral journey I am about to undertake will be correctly understood and generously approved, so that it may further the spiritual good of believers and the cause of peace in the South Atlantic.

Before concluding his meeting with the faithful in St. Peter's Square, the Holy Father announced his pilgrimage to Argentina in the following statement.

Another piece of information: I have received news that my desire to go to Argentina has been welcomed with gratitude and deep satisfaction by the bishops and the supreme authorities of the nation and the Argentine people. The departure date for this pastoral journey is scheduled for the coming June 10th.

Urgent Need Now of Reconciliation

At the London airport at Gatwick the Holy Father delivered the first address of his pilgrimage to Great Britain. It was 8 AM on Friday morning, May 28, 1982. After an address of welcome by Cardinal Hume, the Pope spoke as follows.

Praised be Jesus Christ!

1. I appreciate very much the cordial welcome expressed by His Grace the Duke of Norfolk in the name of Her Majesty the Queen. And with gratitude to God for the opportunity of being among you in the days ahead, I extend to all the people of Britain my greetings of friendship and peace.

You know that I have come on this pilgrimage of faith in order to make a pastoral visit to the Catholic Church here. Preparations for the journey began a long time ago, and I have been looking forward with joyful anticipation to the opportunity of celebrating the Eucharist and the other sacraments with the Catholic faithful of the local Churches. I am also grateful for the ecumenical encounters which will take place during this journey of faith. The promotion of Christian unity is of great importance, for it corresponds to the will of our Lord and Savior Jesus Christ. The sign of unity among all Christians is likewise the way and instrument of effective evangelization. It is, therefore, my fervent prayer that the Lord will bless our efforts to fulfill His will: *Ut omnes unum sint*—"that they may all be one" (Jn. 17:21).

2. My visit is taking place at a time of tension and anxiety, a time when the attention of the world has been focused on the delicate situation of the conflict

in the South Atlantic. During the past weeks, there have been attempts at settling the dispute through diplomatic negotiations, but despite the sincere efforts of many, the situation has developed into one of armed confrontation. It has claimed numerous lives and has even threatened to expand to still more dreadful proportions. This tragic situation has been one of most serious concern to me, and I have repeatedly asked Catholics throughout the world and all people of good will to join me in praying for a just and peaceful settlement. I have also appealed to the authorities of the nations involved, to the Secretary General of the United Nations and to other influential statesmen. In each case I have sought to encourage a solution which would avoid violence and bloodshed. As I stand here today, I renew my heartfelt appeal and I pray that such a settlement of the dispute will soon be reached.

3. At this moment of history, we stand in urgent need of reconciliation: reconciliation between nations and between peoples of different races and cultures; reconciliation of man within himself and with nature; reconciliation among people of different social conditions and beliefs, reconciliation among Christians. In a world scarred by hatred and injustice and divided by violence and oppression, the Church desires to be a spokesman for the vital task of fostering harmony and unity and forging new bonds of understanding and brotherhood.

And so I begin my pastoral visit to Britain with the words of our Lord Jesus Christ: "Peace be with you." May the God of peace and reconciliation be with you all. May He bless your families and homes with His deep and abiding peace.

I Come at the Service of Unity in Love

After the welcome ceremony at the airport the Holy Father went to the cathedral in Westminster where he concelebrated Mass with the bishops of England and Wales, in the course of which he conferred the Sacraments of Baptism and Confirmation on five adults. During the Mass he delivered the following homily.

"Lord, you know everything: you know that I love you!"

My brothers and sisters,

1. With heartfelt gratitude and love I thank our Lord and Savior Jesus Christ, that He has given me the grace of coming among you today. *Today, for the first time in history, a Bishop of Rome sets foot on English soil.* I am deeply moved at this thought. This fair land, once a distant outpost of the pagan world, has become, through the preaching of the Gospel, a beloved and gifted portion of Christ's vineyard.

Yours is a tradition embedded in the history of Christian civilization. The roll of your saints and of your great men and women, your treasures of literature and music, your cathedrals and colleges, your rich heritage of parish life speak of a tradition of faith. And it is to the faith of your fathers—living still—that I wish to pay tribute by my visit.

I am happy that I can concelebrate this Eucharist with my brother bishops who, together with me, are the successors of the Apostles, and whose task it is to sanctify and govern the portion of the Church entrusted to their pastoral care (cf. LG 19).

2. Let us reflect on the spiritual significance of this moment.

Christ, "the chief Shepherd" (1 Pt. 5:4), gave to Peter—as we have heard proclaimed in the passage from St. John's Gospel—the task of confirming his brothers in their faith and in their pastoral duty: "Feed my lambs.... Look after my sheep" (Jn. 21:15-16).

I come among you in response to this command of the Lord. I come to confirm the faith of my brother bishops. I come to remind all believers who today inherit the faith of their fathers that in each diocese the bishop is the visible sign and source of the Church's unity. I come among you as the visible sign and source of unity for the whole Church. I come at the service of unity in love: in the humble and realistic love of the repentant fisherman: "Lord, you know everything; you know that I love you."

Christians down the ages often traveled to that city where the Apostles Peter and Paul had died in witness to their faith and were buried. But, during four hundred years the steady flow of English pilgrims to the tombs of the Apostles shrank to a trickle. Rome and your country were estranged. Now the Bishop of Rome comes to you. I truly come at the service of unity in love, but I come as a friend, too, and I am deeply grateful for your welcome.

I have always admired your love of freedom, your generous hospitality to other peoples in their adversity; as a son of Poland I have the strongest, most personal reason for this admiration and for the thanks that go with it.

3. With these sentiments, I am especially glad to do what Peter did in the early Church. I shall administer Baptism here this morning and meditate with you on its meaning.

In a mysterious but real way, there is repeated and re-presented in this hallowed place that moment of the early Church's life when, as we have read in the Acts of the Apostles, "Peter stood with the Eleven and addressed them in a loud voice" (Acts 2:14) concerning the need to be baptized and to receive the gift of the Holy Spirit. As a result many "received his word" and were baptized, being added to the number of the household of the living God.

4. Through Baptism we are incorporated into Christ. We accept His promise and His commands.

The meaning of Baptism is reflected in the symbolism of the sacramental rite. Water, washing over us, speaks of the redeeming power of Christ's suffering, death and resurrection, washing away the inheritance of sin, delivering us from a kingdom of darkness into a kingdom of light and love. By Baptism we are indeed immersed into the death of Christ—baptized, as St. Paul says, into His death—so as to rise with Him in His resurrection (cf. Rom. 6:3-5). The anointing of our heads with oil signifies how we are strengthened in the power of Christ and become living temples of the Holy Spirit.

We are on the eve of Pentecost, the feast of the Holy Spirit who descends on us at Baptism. One of the finest passages in the Pentecost liturgy was written by an Englishman, Stephen Langton, an Archbishop of Canterbury. In six short and vivid lines he calls upon the Holy Spirit to work in us:

> Wash what is unclean.
> Water what is parched.
> Heal what is diseased.
> Bend what is rigid.

Warm what is cold.
Straighten what is crooked.

Most of the ills of our age or of any age can be brought under that prayer. It reflects a boundless confidence in the power of the Spirit whom it invokes.

5. Through Baptism we are incorporated into the Church. The minister, our parents and godparents sign us with the Sign of the Cross, Christ's proud standard. This shows that it is the whole assembly of the faithful, the whole community of Christ, that supports us in the new life of faith and obedience that follows from our Baptism, our new birth in Christ.

In Baptism we are drawn into the community of faith. We become part of the pilgrim People of God which, in all times and in all places, goes forward in hope towards the fulfillment of the "promise." It is our task to take our place responsibly and lovingly beside those who, from the beginning, "remained faithful to the teaching of the apostles, to the brotherhood, to the breaking of bread and to the prayers" (Acts 2:42).

6. Baptism creates a sacramental bond of unity linking all who have been reborn by means of it. But Baptism, of itself, is only a beginning, a point of departure, for it is wholly directed towards the fullness of life in Christ (cf. UR 22). Baptism is the foundation of the unity that all Christians have in Christ: a unity we must seek to perfect. When we set out clearly the privilege and the duty of the Christian, we feel ashamed that we have not all been capable of maintaining the full unity of faith and charity that Christ willed for His Church.

We the baptized have work to do together as brothers and sisters in Christ. The world is in need of Jesus Christ and His Gospel—the Good News that God loves us, that God the Son was born, was crucified and died to save us, that He rose again and that we rose with Him, and that in Baptism He has sealed us with the Spirit for the first time, gathered us into a community of love and of witness to His truth.

These are my thoughts as we gather to celebrate the Sacrament of Baptism in this historic place. This fine church where we meet is a symbol of the faith and energy of the English Catholic community in modern times. Its architecture is unusual for this country: it evokes memories of other parts of the Christian world, reminding us of our universality. Tomorrow I shall be welcomed in the much older cathedral of Canterbury, where St. Augustine, sent by my Predecessor St. Gregory, first built a little church whose foundations remain. There indeed everything speaks of ancient common traditions, which, in this modern age, we are ready to stress together. I, too, want to speak in this way—to mourn the long estrangement between Christians, to hear gladly our blessed Lord's prayer and command that we should be completely one, to thank Him for that inspiration of the Holy Spirit which has filled us with a longing to leave behind our divisions and aspire to a common witness to our Lord and Savior. My deep desire, my ardent hope and prayer is that my visit may serve the cause of Christain unity.

7. I would like to recall another aspect of Baptism which is perhaps the most universally familiar. In Baptism we are given a name—we call it our Christian name. In the tradition of the Church it is a saint's

name, a name of one of the heroes among Christ's followers—an apostle, a martyr, a religious founder, like St. Benedict, whose monks founded Westminster Abbey nearby, where your sovereigns are crowned. Taking such names reminds us again that we are being drawn into the communion of saints, and at the same time that great models of Christian living are set before us. London is particularly proud of two outstanding saints, great men also by the world's standards, contributors to your national heritage, John Fisher and Thomas More.

John Fisher, the Cambridge scholar of Renaissance learning, became bishop of Rochester. He is an example to all bishops in his loyalty to the Faith and in his devoted attention to the people of his diocese, especially the poor and the sick. Thomas More was a model layman living the Gospel to the full. He was a fine scholar and an ornament to his profession, a loving husband and father, humble in prosperity, courageous in adversity, humorous and godly. Together they served God and their country—bishop and layman. Together they died, victims of an unhappy age. Today we have the grace, all of us, to proclaim their greatness and to thank God for giving such men to England.

In this England of fair and generous minds, no one will begrudge the Catholic community pride in its own history. So I speak last of another Christian name, less famous but no less deserving honor. Bishop Richard Challoner guided the Catholics of this London district in the eighteenth century, at what seemed the lowest point of their fortunes. They were few. It seemed they might well not survive. Yet Bishop

Challoner bravely raised his voice to prophesy a better future for his people. And now, two centuries later, I am privileged to stand here and to speak to you, in no triumphal spirit, but as a friend, grateful for your kind welcome and full of love for all of you.

Bishop Challoner's courage may remind all of us where the seeds of courage lie, where the confidence of renewal comes from. It is through water and the Holy Spirit that a new people is born, whatever the darkness of the time.

8. As the reading from the prophet Ezekiel reminds us, it is the Lord Himself who is the true Shepherd of this new people. He Himself pastures His sheep. He shows them where to rest: "As a shepherd keeps all his flock in view...so shall I keep my sheep in view. I shall rescue them from wherever they have been scattered during the mist and the darkness.... I shall look for the lost one, bring back the stray, bandage the wounded and make the weak strong" (Ez. 34:12, 16).

May those of us who today renew our baptismal vows, as well as those who are now to be baptized, cry out and raise our plea to our heavenly Father through Jesus Christ His Son, our Lord:

"O Shepherd of Israel, hear us...implore,
O Lord, come to our help.

God of hosts, turn again, look down from heaven and see.

Visit this vine and protect it,
the vine your right hand has planted.

And we shall never forsake you again:
give us life that we may call upon your name" (Ps. 80:1-2, 14-15, 18). Amen.

My dear brothers and sisters, as we proceed to celebrate the mysteries of our faith, we cannot forget that an armed conflict is taking place.

Brothers in Christ are fighting in a war that imperils peace in the world.

In our prayers let us remember the victims of both sides. We pray for the dead—that they may rest in Christ—and for the wounded, and for all the afflicted families. I ask you to join me at each step of my pastoral visit, praying for a peaceful solution of the conflict, praying that the God of peace will move men's hearts to put aside the weapons of death, and to pursue the path of fraternal dialogue. With all our heart we turn to Jesus the Prince of Peace.

The Value of Suffering

After meeting Queen Elizabeth II at Buckingham Palace in the afternoon of May 28, the Holy Father presided at a para-liturgical ceremony for the sick in Southwark Cathedral. During the long and moving meeting with the sick, the Pope gave the following discourse.

My brothers and sisters,

1. Praised be Jesus Christ! Praised be Jesus Christ who invites us to share in His life through our Baptism. Praised be Jesus Christ who calls us to unite our sufferings to His so that we may be one with Him in giving glory to the Father in heaven.

Today I greet you in the name of Jesus. I thank all of you for the welcome you have given me. I want you to know how I have looked forward to this meeting with you, especially with those of you who are sick, disabled or infirm. I myself have had a share in suffering and I have known the physical weakness that comes with injury and sickness.

2. It is precisely because I have experienced suffering that I am able to affirm with ever greater conviction what St. Paul says in the second reading: "Neither death, nor life, nor angels, nor principalities, nor things present, nor things to come, nor powers, nor height, nor depth, nor anything else in all creation, will be able to separate us from the love of God in Christ Jesus our Lord" (Rom. 8:38-39).

Dear friends, there is no force or power that can block God's love for you. Sickness and suffering seem to contradict all that is worthy, all that is desired by man. And yet no disease, no injury, no infirmity can ever deprive you of your dignity as children of God, as brothers and sisters of Jesus Christ.

3. By His dying on the cross, Christ shows us how to make sense of our suffering. In His passion we find the inspiration and strength to turn away from any temptation to resentment and grow through pain into new life.

Suffering is an invitation to be more like the Son in doing the Father's will. It offers us an opportunity to imitate Christ who died to redeem mankind from sin. Thus the Father has disposed that suffering can enrich the individual and the whole Church.

4. We acknowledge that the Anointing of the Sick is for the benefit of the whole person. We find this point demonstrated in the liturgical texts of the sacramental celebration: "Make this oil a remedy for all who are anointed with it; heal them in body, in soul and in spirit, and deliver them from every affliction."

The anointing is therefore a source of strength for both the soul and the body. The prayer of the Church asks that sin and the remnants of sin be taken away (cf. DS 1969). It also implores a restoration of health, but always in order that bodily healing may bring greater union with God through the increase of grace.

In her teaching on this sacrament, the Church passes on the truth contained in our first reading from St. James: "Is any among you sick? Let him call for the elders of the Church and let them pray over him, anointing him with oil in the name of the Lord; and the prayer of faith will save the sick man, and the

Lord will raise him up; and if he has committed sins, he will be forgiven" (Jas. 5:14-15).

5. This sacrament should be approached in a spirit of great confidence, like the leper in the Gospel that has just been proclaimed. Even the desperateness of the man's condition did not stop him from approaching Jesus with trust. We too must believe in Christ's healing love and reaffirm that nothing will separate us from that love. Surely Jesus wishes to say: "I will; be clean" (Mt. 8:3); be healed; be strong; be saved.

My dear brothers and sisters, as you live the passion of Christ you strengthen the Church by the witness of your faith. You proclaim by your patience, your endurance and your joy the mystery of Christ's redeeming power. You will find the crucified Lord in the midst of your sickness and suffering.

6. As Veronica ministered to Christ on His way to Calvary, so Christians have accepted the care of those in pain and sorrow as privileged opportunities to minister to Christ Himself. I commend and bless all those who work for the sick in hospitals, residential homes and centers of care for the dying. I would like to say to you doctors, nurses, chaplains and all other hospital staff: Yours is a noble vocation. Remember, it is Christ to whom you minister in the sufferings of your brothers and sisters.

7. I support with all my heart those who recognize and defend the law of God which governs human life. We must never forget that every person, from the moment of conception to the last breath, is a unique child of God and has a right to life. This right should be defended by the attentive care of the medical and

nursing professions and by the protection of the law. Every human life is willed by our heavenly Father and is a part of His loving plan.

No state has the right to contradict moral values which are rooted in the nature of man himself. These values are the precious heritage of civilization. If society begins to deny the worth of any individual or to subordinate the human person to pragmatic or utilitarian considerations, it begins to destroy the defenses that safeguard its own fundamental values.

8. Today I make an urgent plea to this nation. Do not neglect your sick and elderly. Do not turn away from the handicapped and the dying. Do not push them to the margins of society. For if you do, you will fail to understand that they represent an important truth. The sick, the elderly, the handicapped and the dying teach us that weakness is a creative part of human living, and that suffering can be embraced with no loss of dignity. Without the presence of these people in your midst you might be tempted to think of health, strength and power as the only important values to be pursued in life. *But the wisdom of Christ and the power of Christ are to be seen in the weakness of those who share His sufferings.*

Let us keep the sick and the handicapped at the center of our lives. Let us treasure them and recognize with gratitude the debt we owe them. We begin by imagining that we are giving to them; we end by realizing that they have enriched us.

May God bless and comfort all who suffer. And may Jesus Christ, the Savior of the world and Healer of the sick, make His light shine through human weakness as a beacon for us and for all mankind. Amen.

32 ENGLAND, SCOTLAND AND WALES: UNITY—GOD'S GIFT

My dear brothers and sisters in Christ, as we speak of suffering, affliction and death, we cannot forget those who have suffered and died during the armed conflict in the South Atlantic. Let us now remember in our prayers the victims of both sides. May the Father of mercies and of all consolation be close to the wounded and to all the families touched by tragedy.

May He give eternal rest to those who have died in Christ and to those who mourn in Christian hope and let us pray that negotiations may pave the way to a just and lasting peace. We ask this through Christ our Lord. Amen.

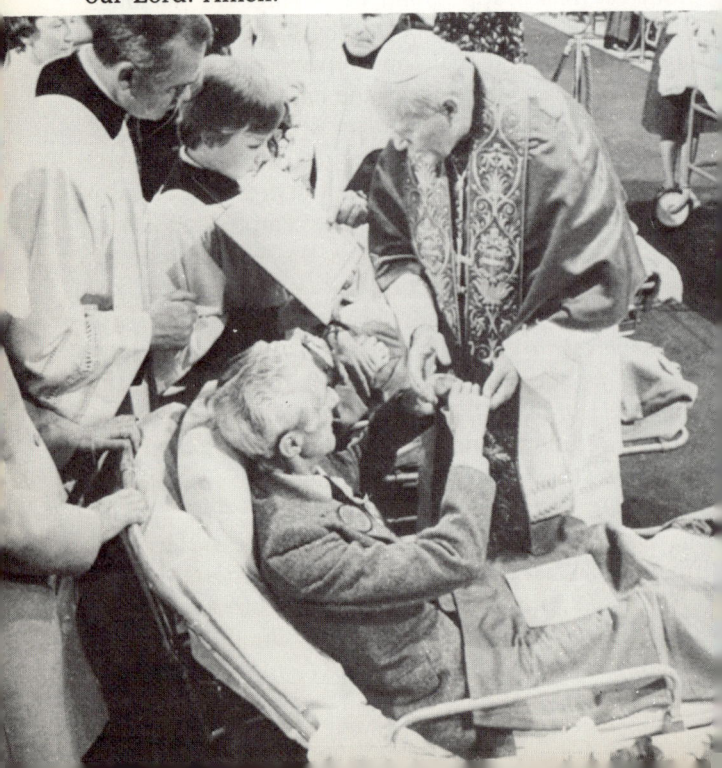

Collaborating for the Good of the Universal Church

Pope John Paul met the bishops of England and Wales on the evening of his first day in England at the residence of Cardinal Hume. After an address by the Cardinal, the Holy Father delivered the following address.

My dear brother bishops,

1. As we come together this evening, we turn our thoughts immediately to our Lord Jesus Christ. In the Gospels, Christ tells us that He is not alone. He experiences communion with His Father: "And he who sent me is with me; he has not left me alone..." (Jn. 8:29). On another occasion He says: "I am not alone, for the Father is with me" (Jn. 16:32). Christ's consciousness of being one with His Father pervades His life and His mission. It is a source of strength for Him. Even at the height of His passion, He knows that He is not abandoned, even though He suffers in His human nature the anguish of loneliness.

2. Christ also knows that His disciples have the very same need as He had: they must not face their mission alone. And so He made His promise, a promise that pervades the life of the whole Church, forever: "I am with you always, to the close of the age" (Mt. 28:20).

This promise was the echo of promises that God had made before. Moses had heard God say: "I will be with you" (Ex. 3:12). It was a promise that was made to him precisely so that he could lead God's people into freedom. Jeremiah, who was to shrink in fear before the magnitude of his prophetic task, was reassured by God: "I am with you to deliver you" (Jer. 1:8). The Apostle Paul, too, heard reassuring words: "Do not be afraid but speak and do not be silent, for I am with you..." (Acts 18:9).

CHRIST IS WITH YOU AND IN YOU

3. And today, in the context of the collegiality that we are celebrating, I wish to offer for your meditation Christ's promise to remain with His Church, Christ's assurance that you are not alone.

The principle of collegiality shows us how Christ's own conviction about Himself—"I am not alone"—applies to ourselves. Through the action of His Holy Spirit, Christ is with you and in you, as you preside, as His vicars (cf. LG 27), over the Churches entrusted to your pastoral care. He is also close to you through the ministry of Him to whom the Church attributes in a special way the titles of Vicar of Christ and Servant of the Servants of God.

4. All of you together, as a conference—the Latin Rite Ordinaries as well as Bishop Hornyak, beloved pastor of the Ukrainian faithful—know the solidarity of the Bishop of Rome with you in prayer and fraternal love. And as members of the world-wide College of Bishops, you know that you have the support of the Successor of the Apostle Peter who was made "a permanent and visible source and foundation of unity of faith and communion," precisely "in order that the episcopate itself might be one and undivided" (LG 18). In the past weeks the Pope has been close to you, as he has been close to your Argentine brothers in the

episcopate, in the great pastoral need that has been experienced by both your peoples as the result of armed conflict in the South Atlantic.

At the same time, you and the bishops of Argentina have been assured of the prayers and fraternal support of your brother bishops throughout the world. The concelebrated Mass in St. Peter's Basilica on May 22 was among other aspects, an example of the powerful collegiality that transcends natural boundaries, languages, cultures and even generations. The appeal for peace made at that time was a collegial act in favor of the whole Church and all humanity. The Episcopal College stands by its individual members. The problems of individual bishops and conferences are, as you have experienced, the concern of the whole body. You are not alone.

COLLABORATION OF THE COLLEGE OF CARDINALS

5. You in your turn are called upon to collaborate for the good of the universal Church. Some of you had the privilege, as I did, of taking part in the Second Vatican Council. All of you have contributed in one way or another to the work of the Synod of Bishops or to that of your episcopal conference. Some of you have taken part in the collegial activities coordinated in the Roman Curia.

6. At the same time the universal episcopate with which you have worked for the good of the whole Church collaborates with the Roman Pontiff in important matters that touch your local Churches. This aspect, too, is a vital part of collegiality: not only do you collaborate for the good of others, but you accept

the collaboration of the College in your own ministry. That collaboration is offered in various ways, often in non-juridical expressions, and it is a great help to you. In this aspect of collegiality you yourselves are helped to read accurately the "signs of the times," to discern clearly "what the Spirit says to the churches" (Rv. 2:7). It is in this context of collegiality that we see how the local Churches and their pastors contribute to the universal Church, and also how they receive the combined insights of the universal episcopate. These insights assist local bishops to be ever more solicitous for the good of the whole Church; they likewise help the bishops to safeguard in their local Churches that unity of faith and discipline which is common to the whole Church (LG 23), and which must be authenticated by her universal authority. In the principle of collegiality, the bishops find at one and the same time fraternal support and a criterion of accountability for their sacred mission. The words of Jesus are certainly full of meaning for us His servants: I am not alone.

7. In your ministry as bishops you know how much your priests depend on you, and how much you depend on your priests. Together—and not alone— you have been commissioned to proclaim the Gospel and build up the Body of Christ. The priests are your brothers and the co-workers of your episcopal order. Your brotherhood with them ensures the effectiveness of your ministry, and their union with you guarantees their union with Christ.

IMPORTANT ROLE

8. Now a word about religious. The Second Vatican Council and its implementing documents have done much to show the genuine place of reli-

gious in the apostolate of the local Churches. Here too your role is so important, not only for the coordination of pastoral activity but also for ensuring that the splendid contribution of men and women religious is adequately utilized in the spirit of shared responsibility for the Gospel, "that the word of the Lord may speed on and triumph" (2 Thes. 3:1). In your pastoral zeal, the orderly and fruitful collaboration between bishops and religious will confirm your own joyful experience of not being alone in the work of evangelization and catechesis.

HEAVY RESPONSIBILITY

9. And what of the laity? I am deeply convinced also that the increased scope of the lay apostolate is a source of special strength for you as pastors of God's People. The Second Vatican Council was emphatic in stating how much the laity contribute to the welfare of the entire Church. In the same context it states that "pastors also know that they themselves were not meant by Christ to shoulder alone the entire saving mission of the Church" (LG 30). In God's plan, by fulfilling their own proper role, the laity are meant to offer a great service of loving support to their pastors in Christ.

In all of this, the task of the bishops remains a formidable one. It is a ministry of heavy responsibility, but the presence of Christ and the right measure of shared responsibility assumed by the community is more than enough to convince us all as bishops that we are not alone.

10. There are so many ways in which we are called to serve as bishops—so many individual areas

of our pastoral mission: as teachers, leading God's People "by right paths for his name's sake" (Ps. 23:3); as leaders of liturgical worship, offering "praise in the vast assembly" (Ps. 35:18); as loving and compassionate shepherds who know their sheep and are known and loved by them. In all these various areas the principle of collegiality finds its pertinent application, and the life and ministry of the bishop is marked by the experience of Christ the chief Shepherd, who proclaims unceasingly to the world: I am not alone.

11. And today, dear bishops, the Bishop of Rome wishes to emphasize this point strongly: that like Christ you are not alone. With you the Bishop of Rome is Pastor of God's People, and for you he is the universal servant pastor. As he confirms you in the Faith, he also encourages you and your people—as well as your Argentine confreres and their people—in every effort for total reconciliation and peace. With the Apostle Peter, I say again: "Peace to all of you that are in Christ" (1 Pt. 5:14).

WE ARE NOT ALONE

And together, my brother bishops—and not alone —we must proclaim that peace is possible, that it is a human and Christian duty, that reconciliation is the way to peace, and that Christ Himself is our justice and our peace. Amidst joys and anxieties, in hopes and pain, the Catholic episcopate is jointly accountable to Jesus Christ for the way in which it proclaims, in His name and by His mandate, His Gospel of peace, and exercises His "ministry of reconciliation" (2 Cor. 5:18).

With our clergy, religious and laity, and united with one another, let us proclaim the saving and reconciling message of the Gospel, with a deep conviction that—like Jesus and with Jesus—we are not alone. In the collegiality of the Catholic episcopate let us find renewed strength and vigor to lead God's People. And in Christ Jesus may we always realize that we are not alone.

The Secular City Has Need of Your Witness

At the Digby Stuart Training College in London, John Paul II met the religious men and women of England and Wales on Saturday morning, May 29. During the meeting he addressed them as follows.

My dear brothers and sisters in Christ,

1. I wish to express my special joy at this meeting. You are here in such large numbers as representatives of all the religious of England and Wales. On the eve of Pentecost you are here to renew your religious vows. With the Pope, the Successor of Peter, you will proclaim before the whole Church that you believe in your consecration; that it is your call to follow Christ which inspires your joy and your peace. "Rejoice in the Lord always" (Phil. 4:4).

AMAZING REBIRTH

2. You worthily continue a tradition that goes back to the dawn of English Christian history. Augustine and his companions were Benedictine monks. The great monastic foundations of Anglo-Saxon and medieval times were not just the staging posts for evangelization; they were also the centers of learning and the seedbeds of culture and civilization. Places such as Canterbury, Jarrow, Glastonbury and Saint Albans are indicative of the role monasticism played in English history. Men like Bede of Jarrow, Boniface of Devon who became the Apostle of the Germans,

and Dunstan of Glastonbury who became Archbishop of Canterbury in 960; women such as Hilda of Whitby, Walburga and Lioba, and many others—these are famous names in English history. Nor can we forget Anselm, or Nicholas Breakspear, born at Abbots Langley, who became Pope Adrian IV in 1154.

In Norman times this army of Christ reached new splendor with the foundation of monasteries of Cistercians, Dominicans, Franciscans, Carmelites and Augustinians.

Later, religious life suffered greatly. English religious communities were scattered and destroyed, or fled to foreign lands. It is impossible here to name all the men and women religious of this period who followed our Lord to the point of giving their lives in defense of their Faith. To that unhappy age belonged also an extraordinary Yorkshire woman, Mary Ward, who became a pioneer of the active unenclosed congregations for women.

The last century saw an amazing rebirth of religious life. Hundreds of religious houses, schools, orphanages, hospitals and other social services were established. Missionary congregations spread the Faith in distant lands.

In our own time the Second Vatican Council has addressed to you a call for appropriate renewal of religious life through a return to the original charism of each institute and through a healthy adaptation to meet the changed conditions of the times (cf. PC 2).

3. My brothers and sisters, we can see what the Church, and indeed society at large, expects from you today. The people of our time look to you and repeat what the Greek-speaking visitors to Jerusalem said to

the Apostle Philip: "We wish to see Jesus" (Jn. 12:21). Yes, *in you the world wishes to see Jesus.* Your public profession of the evangelical counsels is a radical response to the Lord's call to follow Him. As a result, your lives are meant to offer a clear witness to the reality of the kingdom of God already present in the affairs of men and nations.

As you renew your religious consecration here this morning before God and the Church, in the sight of millions of your fellow countrymen, I wish to meditate with you on the greatness and dignity of your calling.

NEWNESS OF LIFE IN CHRIST

4. To most people you are known for what you do. Visitors to your abbeys and religious houses see you celebrate the Liturgy, or follow you in prayer and contemplation. People of all ages and conditions benefit directly from your many different services to ecclesial and civil society. You teach; you care for the sick; you look after the poor, the old, the handicapped; you bring the Word of God to those near and far; you lead the young to human and Christian maturity.

5. Most people know what you do, and admire and appreciate you for it. Your true greatness, though, comes from what you are. Perhaps what you are is less known and understood. In fact, what you are can only be grasped in the light of the "newness of life" revealed by the risen Lord. In Christ you are a "new creation" (cf. 2 Cor. 5:17).

At some time in your lives, the call of the Lord to a special intimacy and union with Him in His redemptive mission became so clear that you overcame your hesitations. You put aside your doubts and difficulties and committed yourselves to a life of total fidelity to the highest ideals of the Gospel. Your free decision was sustained by grace, and your perseverance through the years is a magnificent testimony of the victory of grace over the forces that struggle to tarnish the newness of your life in Christ. This "newness of life" is a gift of Christ to His Church. It is a proof of the Church's holiness, an expression of her vitality.

6. Through the profession of the evangelical counsels you are bound to the Church in a special way (cf. LG 44). Let me suggest to you, then, some of the aspects of your consecrated life that are especially significant in the present circumstances of the pilgrim People of God. Today there exists a widespread temptation to unbelief and despair. You, on the other hand are committed to being men and women of deep faith and unceasing prayer. To you in a particular way may be addressed St. Paul's exhortation to Timothy: "Fight the good fight of the faith: take hold of the eternal life to which you were called when you made the good confession in the presence of many witnesses" (1 Tm. 6:12). Believe in the risen Lord. Believe in your own personal vocation. Believe that Christ called you because He loves you. In moments of darkness and pain, believe that He loves you all the more. Believe in the specific inspiration and charism of your institute. Believe in your mission within the Church. Let your faith shine before the world, as a lamp in the darkness; let it shine as a beacon that will guide a confused society to the proper appreciation of essential values. May the spiritual joy of your personal lives

and your communal witness of authentic Christian love be sources of inspiration and hope. Let your consecration be known. Be recognizable as religious men and women. The secular city needs living witnesses such as you.

COMPLETE DEDICATION

7. Today many people are tempted to live by a false set of values. You, on the other hand, are men and women who have discovered the pearl of great price (cf. Mt. 13:46), a treasure that does not fail (cf. Lk. 12:22-34). Through poverty voluntarily embraced in imitation of Christ—being poor in spirit and in fact, singly and corporately (cf. PC 13)—you seek freedom from the tyranny of the consumer society. Chastity practiced "for the sake of the kingdom of heaven" (Mt. 19:12) is a special gift to you from Christ, and from you to the whole Church. Virginity or celibacy is not only a preferential love of the Lord, but also a freedom for a total self-giving in universal service, without conditions and without discrimination. Your chastity, when it is marked by genuine generosity and joy, teaches others to distinguish between true love and its many counterfeits. Through your obedience, which is a complete dedication of yourselves to the will of God, you seek to achieve the "mature measure of the stature of the fullness of Christ" (Eph. 4:13). Paradoxically, through self-renunciation, you grow to human and Christian maturity and responsibility. You show that many current ideas of freedom are in fact distorted. You help ransom society, as it were, from the effects of unbridled selfishness.

8. The witness of religious consecration has a special dimension for those of you who live the con-

templative form of religious life. Your lives are hidden with Christ in God. In silence and through prayer and penance you praise Him. You call down His graces and blessings upon God's People (cf. PC 7). Many people have a vague idea of what you do, but very many more, including Catholics, fail to recognize the greatness of your special vocation and its irreplaceable role in the Church's life. Contemplative life imparts to God's People "a hidden apostolic fruitfulness" *(ibid.)*. Contemplative prayer sustains the Church in her struggle to bring mankind to a proper understanding of human dignity and spiritual values. In the name of the Church I thank you. I ask you to pray all the more for the pilgrim People of God and for the world. And to those who feel called to the contemplative life, I repeat Jesus' invitation to two hesitant disciples: "Come and see." They came and saw and stayed with Him (cf. Jn. 1:39).

GENEROUS FOLLOWERS OF CHRIST

9. The "hidden witness" of contemplatives is flanked by the vigorous apostolic thrust of the active religious communities. In the footsteps of the Master, with zeal for His Father's will, and confident in your own particular charism, you "show wonderfully at work within the Church the surpassing greatness of the force of Christ the King and the boundless power of the Holy Spirit" (LG 44).

Religious communities have a special responsibility to be sensitive to the signs of the times, and to try to meet such needs as are the proper concern of the Church's ministry. Imitate the faith and courage of your founders. Be ready to sacrifice yourselves as they did. Help the bishops in their pastoral ministry, with confidence in Christ's promise to protect and guide His Church.

10. Men and women religious, lift up your hearts! Give thanks to the Lord for your wonderful vocation. Through you Jesus wants to continue His prayer of contemplation on the mountain. He wants to be seen announcing God's kingdom, healing the sick, bringing sinners to conversion, blessing children, doing good to all, and always obeying the will of the Father who sent Him (cf. LG 46). In you the Church and the world must be able to see the living Lord.

Do not be afraid to proclaim openly before the rest of the Church, especially the young, the worthwhileness of your way of life and its beauty. The Catholic community must be shown the high privilege of following Christ's call to the religious life. The young must come to know you more closely. They will come to you when they see you as generous and cheerful followers of Jesus Christ, whose way of life does not offer material rewards and accomodate itself to the standards of the world. They will be attracted by Christ's uncompromising, exciting challenge to leave all in order to follow Him.

11. In concluding, I wish to greet the religious of the Anglican Communion who are present here. You, too, are inspired by the evangelical call to an ever closer following of Christ. You have expressed a desire to welcome the Pope and to hear him speak. I thank you. I commend to your prayers the ardent desire of millions of Christians throughout the world: that we may be fully one in faith and love.

To all of you I express my gratitude and respect. I entrust all the religious of England and Wales to the loving protection of Mary, Mother of the Church, the loftiest example of discipleship. May the Holy Spirit fill your hearts with His gifts. Rejoice in the Lord always! Again, I say, rejoice! May the public renewal of your religious vows help bring about a new Pentecost in your lives and in the Church in this land.

Praised be Jesus Christ!

The Richness of What We Share

Address of Archbishop Runcie

At the beginning of the ecumenical service in Canterbury Cathedral, Archbishop Robert Runcie addressed Pope John Paul II as follows:

Witamy Jego Swiatobliwosc, drogiego Brata w Chrystusie, w imie Pana naszego Jezusa Chrystusa.

We welcome you, Your Holiness, with words of friendship, for this is a service of celebration. But the present moment is full of pain for so many in the world. Millions are hungry and the secret gift of life is counted cheap, while the nations of the world use some of their best resources and much of their store of human ingenuity in refining weapons of death. With so much to celebrate in life and so much to be done to combat life's enemies, disease and ignorance, energy is being wasted in conflict. Our minds inevitably turn to the conflict and tragic loss of life in the South Atlantic and we also remember the suffering of Your Holiness' own fellow countrymen in Poland.

But Christians do not accept hunger, disease and war as inevitable. The present moment is not empty of hope, but waits to be transformed by the power which comes from remembering our beginnings and by a power which comes from a lively vision of the future. Remembering our beginnings, celebrating our hope for the future, freeing ourselves from cynicism and despair in order to act in the present. It is this style of Christian living which gives shape to this service. Every Christian service contains this element of remembering the beginnings of our community when our Lord walked this earth.

At this season of the year we particularly remember the gift of the Holy Spirit at the first Pentecost, and the sending out of the Apostles to carry the Faith of Jesus Christ to the farthest ends of the world. We recall one of the first missionary endeavors of the Roman Church and its efforts to recapture for Christ a Europe overwhelmed by the barbarians. In the year 597, in the words of the English historian the Venerable Bede, Your Holiness' great Predecessor Gregory, prompted by divine inspiration sent a servant of God named Augustine and several more God-fearing monks with him to preach the Word of God to the English race. Augustine became the first Archbishop of Canterbury and I rejoice that the successors of Gregory and Augustine stand here today in the church which is built on the partnership in the Gospel.

We shall trace and celebrate our beginnings in this service, by reaffirming our baptismal vows, made at the font at the beginning of the Christian life, and by saying together the Creed, an expression of the heart of our common Christian faith, composed in the era before our unhappy division. The emphasis then will be on the richness of what we share and upon the existing unity of the Christian Church, which transcends all political divisions and frontiers imposed on the human family.

One of the gifts which Christians have to make to the peace of the world is to live out the unity that has already been given to them in their common love of Christ. But our unity is not in the past only, but also in the future. We have a common vision which also breaks up the lazy prejudices and easy assumptions of the present. Our chapel here of the martyrs of the 20th century will be the focus for the celebration of a common vision. We believe even in a world like ours which exalts and applauds self-interest and derides self-sacrifice that the blood of the martyrs shall create the holy places of the earth.

Our own century has seen the creation of ruthless tyranny by the use of violence, and cynical disregard of truth. We believe that such energies founded on force and lies destroy themselves. The kingdom spoken of by our Lord Jesus Christ is built by self-sacrificing love which can even turn places of sorrow and suffering into signs of hope.

We think of Your Holiness' own fellow countryman, the priest Maximilian Kolbe, who died in place of another in the hell of Auschwitz. We remember with gratitude our own brother Archbishop Yananillewol in Uganda who worked in the worst conditions for Christ's kingdom of love and justice, and whose death inspires us still and will mark the future more deeply than the lives of his oppressors. We remember all the martyrs of our century of martyrs who have confirmed Christ's Church in the conviction that even in the places of horror, the concentration camps, and prisons and slums of the world, nothing in all creation can separate us from the active and creative love of God in Christ Jesus our Lord.

THE RICHNESS OF WHAT WE SHARE 51

If we remember that beginning in Christ Jesus our Lord, if we can face the suffering of traveling in His way, if we can lift our eyes beyond the historic quarrels which have tragically disfigured Christ's Church and wasted so much Christian energy, then we shall indeed enter into a faith worthy of celebration, because it is able to remake the world. Thanks be to God.

Pray and Work for Reconciliation and Unity

The ecumenical ceremony in Canterbury Cathedral was held on the morning of the Pope's second day in Great Britain. During the celebration at which the Holy Father and Dr. Robert Runcie, Primate of the Anglican Communion presided, the Pope gave the following address.

1. The passage which has just been read is taken from the Gospel according to John and contains the words of our Lord Jesus Christ on the eve of His passion. While He was at supper with His disciples, He prayed: "that they may all be one; even as you, Father, are in me, and I in you, that they also may be in us, so that the world may believe that you have sent me" (Jn. 17:21).

These words are marked in a particular way by the Paschal Mystery of our Savior, by His passion, death and resurrection. Though pronounced once only, they endure throughout all generations. Christ prays unceasingly for the unity of His Church, because He loves her with the same love with which He loved the Apostles and disciples who were with Him at the Last Supper. "I do not pray for these only, but also for those who believe in me through their word" (Jn. 17:20). Christ reveals a divine perspective in which the Father and the Son and the Holy Spirit are present. Present also is the most profound mystery of the Church: the unity in love which exists between the Father and the Son and the Holy Spirit penetrates to the heart of the people whom God has chosen to be His own, and is the source of their unity.

Christ's words resound in a special way today in this hallowed cathedral which recalls the figure of the great missionary Saint Augustine whom Pope Gregory the Great sent forth so that through his words the sons and daughters of England might believe in Christ.

Dear brethren, all of us have become particularly sensitive to these words of the priestly prayer of Christ. The Church of our time is the Church which participates in a particular way in the prayer of Christ for unity and which seeks the ways of unity, obedient to the Spirit who speaks in the words of the Lord. We desire to be obedient, especially today, on this historic day which centuries and generations have awaited. We desire to be obedient to Him whom Christ calls the Spirit of truth.

2. On the feast of Pentecost last year Catholics and Anglicans joined with Orthodox and Protestants, both in Rome and in Constantinople, in commemorating the First Council of Constantinople by professing their common faith in the Holy Spirit, the Lord and Giver of life. Once again on this vigil of the great feast of Pentecost, we are gathered in prayer to implore our heavenly Father to pour out anew the Holy Spirit, the Spirit of Christ, upon His Church. For it is the Church which, in the words of that Council's Creed, we profess to be the work par excellence of the Holy Spirit when we say, "we believe in one, holy, catholic and apostolic Church."

Today's Gospel passages have called attention in particular to two aspects of the gift of the Holy Spirit which Jesus invoked upon His disciples: He is the Spirit of truth and the Spirit of unity. On the first Pentecost day, the Holy Spirit descended on that small band of disciples to confirm them in the truth of God's salvation of the world through the death and resurrection of His Son, and to unite them into the one Body of Christ, which is the Church. Thus we know that when we pray "that all may be one" as Jesus and His Father are one, it is precisely in order that "the world may believe" and by this faith be saved (cf. Jn. 17:21). For our faith can be none other than the faith of Pentecost, the faith in which the Apostles were confirmed by the Spirit of truth. We believe that the risen Lord has authority to save us from sin and the powers of darkness. We believe, too, that we are called to "become one body, one spirit in Christ" (Eucharistic Prayer III).

JOINED BY THE SACRAMENT OF BAPTISM

3. In a few moments we shall renew our baptismal vows together. We intend to perform this ritual, which we share in common as Anglicans and Catholics, as a clear testimony to the one Sacrament of Baptism by which we have been joined to Christ. At the same time we are humbly mindful that the Faith of the Church to which we appeal is not without the marks of our separation. Together we shall renew our renunciation of sin in order to make it clear that we believe that Jesus Christ has overcome the powerful hold of Satan upon "the world" (Jn. 14:17). We shall profess anew our intention to turn away from all that is evil and turn towards God who is the Author of all

that is good and the Source of all that is holy. As we again make our profession of faith in the triune God—Father, Son and Holy Spirit—we find great hope in the promise of Jesus: "The Counselor, the Holy Spirit, whom the Father will send in my name, he will teach you all things, and bring to your remembrance all that I have said to you" (Jn. 14:26). Christ's promise gives us confidence in the power of this same Holy Spirit to heal the divisions introduced into the Church in the course of the centuries since that first Pentecost day. In this way the renewal of our baptismal vows will become a pledge to do all in our power to cooperate with the grace of the Holy Spirit, who alone can lead us to the day when we will profess the fullness of our faith together.

4. We can be confident in addressing our prayer for unity to the Holy Spirit today, for according to Christ's promise the Spirit, the Counselor, will be with us forever (cf. Jn. 14:16). It was with confidence that Archbishop Fisher made bold to visit Pope John XXIII at the time of the Second Vatican Council, and that Archbishops Ramsey and Coggan came to visit Pope Paul VI. It is with no less confidence that I have responded to the promptings of the Holy Spirit to be with you today at Canterbury.

COMMON INHERITANCE

5. My dear brothers and sisters of the Anglican Communion, "whom I love and long for" (Phil. 4:1), how happy I am to be able to speak directly to you today in this great cathedral! The building itself is an eloquent witness both to our long years of common inheritance and to the sad years of division that fol-

lowed. Beneath this roof St. Thomas Becket suffered martyrdom. Here too we recall Augustine and Dunstan and Anselm and all those monks who gave such diligent service in this church. The great events of salvation history are retold in the ancient stained glass windows above us. And we have venerated here the manuscript of the Gospels sent from Rome to Canterbury thirteen hundred years ago. Encouraged by the witness of so many who have professed their faith in Jesus Christ through the centuries—often at the cost of their own lives—a sacrifice which even today is asked of not a few, as the new chapel we shall visit reminds us—I appeal to you in this holy place, all my fellow Christians, and especially the members of the Church of England and the members of the Anglican Communion throughout the world, to accept the commitment to which Archbishop Runcie and I pledge ourselves anew before you today. This commitment is that of praying and working for reconciliation and ecclesial unity according to the mind and heart of our Savior Jesus Christ.

I COME IN LOVE

6. On this first visit of a Pope to Canterbury, I come to you in love—the love of Peter to whom the Lord said, "I have prayed for you that your faith may not fail; and when you have turned again, strengthen your brethren" (Lk. 22:32). I come to you also in the love of Gregory, who sent St. Augustine to this place to give the Lord's flock a shepherd's care (cf. 1 Pt. 5:2). Just as every minister of the Gospel must do, so today I echo the words of the Master: "I am among you as one who serves" (Lk. 22:27). With me I bring

to you, beloved brothers and sisters of the Anglican Communion, the hopes and the desires, the prayers and good will of all who are united with the Church of Rome, which from earliest times was said to "preside in love" (Ignatius, *Ad Rom.*, Proem.).

7. In a few moments Archbishop Runcie will join me in signing a *Common Declaration,* in which we give recognition to the steps we have already taken along the path of unity, and state the plans we propose and the hopes we entertain for the next stage of our common pilgrimage. And yet these hopes and plans will come to nothing if our striving for unity is not rooted in our union with God; for Jesus said, "In that day you will know that I am in my Father, and you in me, and I in you. He who has my commandments and keeps them, he it is who loves me; and he who loves me will be loved by my Father, and I will love him and manifest myself to him" (Jn. 14:20-21). This love of God is poured out upon us in the person of the Holy Spirit, the Spirit of truth and of unity. Let us open ourselves to His powerful love, as we pray that, speaking the truth in love, we may all grow up in every way into Him who is the Head, into our Lord Jesus Christ (cf. Eph. 4:15). May the dialogue we have begun lead us to the day of full restoration of unity in faith and love.

SPIRIT OF TRUTH

8. On the eve of His passion, Jesus told His disciples: "If you love me, you will keep my commandments" (Jn. 14:15). We have felt compelled to come together here today in obedience to the great commandment: the commandment of love. We wish

to embrace it in its entirety, to live by it completely, and to experience the power of this commandment in conformity with the words of the Master: "I will pray the Father, and he will give you another Counselor, to be with you forever, the Spirit of truth, whom the world cannot receive, because it neither sees him nor knows him; you know him, for he dwells with you, and will be in you" (Jn. 14:16-17).

Love grows by means of truth, and truth draws near to man by means of love. Mindful of this, I lift up to the Lord this prayer: O Christ, may all that is part of today's encounter be born of the Spirit of truth and be made fruitful through love.

Behold before us: the past and the future!

Behold before us: the desires of so many hearts!

You, who are the Lord of history and the Lord of human hearts, be with us! Christ Jesus, eternal Son of God, be with us! Amen.

Hopes for Growth of Christians into Deeper Communion

At the close of the ecumenical celebration in Canterbury Cathedral, Primatial See of the Anglican Communion, John Paul II met the heads of other Christian Churches and members of the British Council of Churches, during which he delivered the following discourse.

Dear brethren in Jesus Christ,

1. This meeting which the Lord has granted us today is one which I deeply appreciate. It is complementary to the service of prayer and praise in which we have just joined in Canterbury Cathedral, and is evidence of the work of reconciliation to which we are all committed. "All this is from God, who through Christ reconciled us to himself and gave us a ministry of reconciliation" (2 Cor. 5:18). "All this is from God" —it is His work we are seeking to do, His will we are trying to fulfill. By Baptism and the degree of common faith we have just been celebrating in the cathedral, He has already established between us a certain communion, a communion that is real even if it is limited. It is indeed a spiritual communion, "the fellowship of the Holy Spirit" (2 Cor. 13:13) whose coming on the Church we shall once again celebrate tomorrow.

DEEPER COMMUNION

2. But such communion in the Spirit cannot and must not remain something abstract. It has to find

expression in the life of our Churches and communities; it has to be sufficiently visible to be even now a witness we give together to our will for Christian unity in a world that is so sadly divided, a world in which peace is imperiled from so many sides. For these reasons it is a joy for me to hear from you of your hopes for the growth of Christians in these countries into deeper communion, a growth to which through God's grace we are all committed, a growth which we all intend to foster whatever the difficulties we may experience. I have been so happy to learn of the cooperation of the Catholic Church not only with individual Churches and Communities but also with many of the initiatives of the British Council of Churches. I am also pleased to know of the relations of confidence between the Catholic bishops and the leaders of other Churches and Communities which do so much to facilitate cooperation in evangelization in those areas in which this is already possible.

3. You have spoken to me frankly of your hopes and of your problems. Clearly in a short and informal meeting like this we cannot discuss everything. It is my hope, and I am sure it is also yours, that our meeting this morning will not be the end of this fruitful exchange but rather a beginning. I would like to think that, before too long, some of you would be prepared to visit Rome together with some representatives of the Episcopal Conferences of Great Britain and to have further conversations with the Secretariat for Promoting Christian Unity and other offices of the Roman Curia. Thus, please God, we should be able to build further on the foundations so happily laid today.

LONGING FOR UNITY

4. Once more I thank you for your courtesy in coming to meet me. I realize that for this purpose you have left an important meeting organized by the British Council of Churches. When you return there, please assure all those taking part that the Pope longs for the day when, in fulfillment of Christ's will, we shall all be one—one with Him and one with each other. God grant that that day may not be long delayed.

"Peace be to the brethren, and love with faith, from God the Father and the Lord Jesus Christ. Grace be with all who love our Lord Jesus Christ with love undying" (Eph. 6:23-24). Amen.

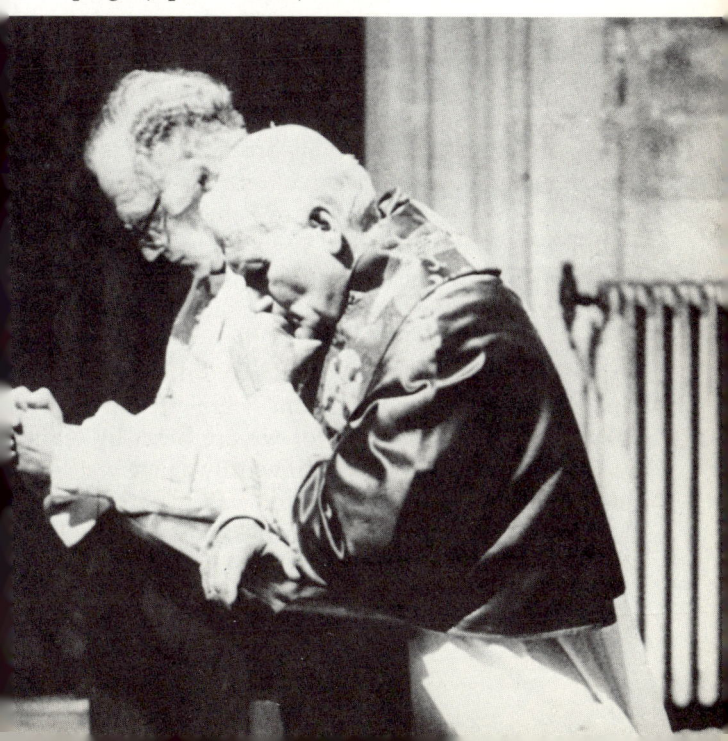

A People That Does the Will of the Heavenly Father

100,000 persons participated on the afternoon of Saturday, May 29, at a Mass celebrated by the Holy Father with 30 bishops, in the stadium at Wembly. In the course of the liturgy, intended especially for the Catholics of southern England, the Pope delivered the following homily.

1. After the ascension the Apostles went back to the Upper Room, where Jesus had instituted the Eucharist and where He had declared that the law of love is the first and most essential of His commandments. And there they "joined in continuous prayer, together with several women, including Mary the mother of Jesus, and with his brothers" (Acts 1:14). This evening we have gathered here in a similar spiritual atmosphere. On the eve of Pentecost I am celebrating this Mass with you. Together we shall renew our baptismal promises as an offering of ourselves to our heavenly Father, joined to the sacrificial offering of Christ in the Eucharist.

Let us reflect together on the Word of God. The Apostles in the Upper Room were afraid. They prayed. And we too pray, for we are beset by fears and weaknesses: "We groan inwardly as we wait for our bodies to be set free"; we too wait in patience for the Spirit to come to help us in our weakness (cf. Rom. 8:22-26).

Unfortunately not all of the Lord's disciples are fully united in faith and charity. This is one of the reasons why I have come to Britain, and why I have made a pilgrimage today to the Cathedral of Canterbury.

But I have come above all to make a pastoral visit to the Catholic community; to visit the Church that is in England and Wales; to renew with you our shared love and enthusiasm for the Gospel of Jesus Christ; to confirm you in your faith and to share your joys and your hopes, your griefs and your anxieties.

FULL OF RESPECT FOR ALL

2. As I look at this great assembly I am full of respect for each of you. You are God's sons and daughters; He loves you. I believe in you. I believe in all mankind. I believe in the unique dignity of every human being. I believe that each individual has a value that can never be ignored or taken away.

Yet I also know that often, too often, human dignity and human rights are not respected. Man is set against man, class against class, in useless conflicts. Immigrants, people of a different color, religion or culture suffer discrimination and hostility. The heart of man is restless and troubled. Man conquers space but is unsure about himself; he is confused about the direction in which he is heading. It is tragic that our technological mastery is greater than our wisdom about ourselves. All this must be changed. "O Lord, the earth is full of your creatures.... When you send forth your Spirit, they are created, and you renew the face of the earth" (Ps. 104:24, 30). Let this be our plea. May we be renewed in the depths of our hearts in the power of the Holy Spirit.

3. Together we shall renew our baptismal promises. We shall reject sin, and the glamor of evil, and Satan, the father of sin and prince of darkness. We shall profess our faith in the one God, in His Son, our Savior Jesus Christ, in the coming of the Holy Spirit, in the Church, in life everlasting. And we shall be responsible for the words we say, and be bound by an alliance with our God.

RECOVER A SENSE OF GOD'S PRESENCE

4. Brothers and sisters! In order to be faithful to this alliance we must be a people of prayer and deep spirituality. Our society needs to recover a sense of God's loving presence, and a renewed sense of respect for His will.

Let us learn this from Mary our Mother. In England, "the Dowry of Mary," the faithful, for centuries, have made pilgrimages to her shrine at Walsingham. Today Walsingham comes to Wembly, and the statue of Our Lady of Walsingham, present here, lifts our minds to meditate on our Mother. She obeyed the will of God fearlessly and gave birth to the Son of God by the power of the Holy Spirit. Faithful at the foot of the cross, she then waited in prayer for the Holy Spirit to descend on the infant Church. It is Mary who will teach us how to be silent, how to listen for the voice of God in the midst of a busy and noisy world. It is Mary who will help us to find time for prayer. Through the rosary, that great Gospel prayer, she will help us to know Christ. We need to live as she did, in the presence of God, raising our minds and hearts to Him in our daily activities and worries.

May your homes become schools of prayer for both parents and children. God should be the living hearth of your family life. Keep Sunday holy. Go to Mass every Sunday. At Mass the People of God gather together in unity around the altar to worship and to intercede. At Mass you exercise the great privilege of your Baptism: to praise God in union with Christ His Son; to praise God in union with His Church.

It is particularly important for you to be united with your bishops. They are the successors of the Apostles; they are the guardians and teachers of the true Faith. Love and respect them and pray for them; they have been given the task of leading you to Christ.

And you, my dear brothers in the ministry of the priesthood, you have a special responsibility. You must build up the Body of Christ. You have to encourage the laity in their particular vocation in society. You have to help them to "put on Christ." You have to support them in their Christian lives and challenge them to ever greater holiness. Open for your people the treasures of the Church's liturgy. Celebrate the Mass with understanding, with reverence and with love. Continue to teach the importance of frequent communion. Encourage regular confession. It is a sacrament of enduring power and importance. Develop in your parishes an atmosphere and a practice of fervent prayer and community life.

WE AWAIT SALVATION

5. Brothers and sisters, to be faithful to our alliance with God we must be not only a people that prays, but also a people that does the will of the heavenly Father. Again it is Mary who teaches us

how. Through her obedience she accepted the whole of God's plan for her life. And in doing so she achieved greatness. "Blessed is she who believed that there would be a fulfillment of what was spoken to her from the Lord" (Lk. 1:45).

We express our real acceptance of Christ's word by respecting the moral demands of our Christian vocation. And the fulfillment of these demands is an act of loving obedience to the person of Jesus Christ the Incarnate Word of God. If our faith is strong, the moral demands of the Christian life—although at times they are difficult to fulfill and although they always require effort and grace—will seem neither unreasonable nor impossible. Certainly, our fidelity to the Gospel will put us at odds with the spirit of the "present age." Yes, we are *in* the world, indeed as disciples of Christ we are *sent into* the world, but we do *not belong* to the world (cf. Jn. 17:16, 18). The conflict between certain values of the world and the values of the Gospel is an inescapable part of the Church's life, just as it is an inescapable part of the life of each one of us. And it is here that we must draw on the "patience" which St. Paul spoke to us about in the second reading. We groan inwardly as we await our salvation, in hope and with patience (cf. Rom. 8:23-25).

MORAL VALUES DECLINING

6. I have often spoken of the decline of respect for the fundamental moral values that are essential to the Christian life. Indeed, moral values are essential to the life of all human beings as free agents created in the image and likeness of God, and destined to a higher creation.

The world has largely lost respect for human life from the moment of conception. It is weak in upholding the indissoluble unity of marriage. It fails to support the stability and holiness of family life. There is a crisis of truth and responsibility in human relationship. Selfishness abounds. Sexual permissiveness and drug addiction ruin the lives of millions of human beings. International relations are fraught with tensions, often because of excessive inequalities and unjust economic, social, cultural and political structures, and because of slowness in applying the needed remedies. Underlying all of this there is often a false concept of man and his unique dignity, and a thirst for power rather than a desire to serve.

Are we Christians to agree with such a state of affairs? Are we to call this progress? Are we to shrug our shoulders and say that nothing can be done to change all this?

My brothers and sisters, the essence of our Christian vocation consists in being "light" and "salt" for the world we live in. Let us not be afraid: "The Spirit comes to help us in our weakness" (Rom. 8:26).

Keep in mind that picture of Mary and the Apostles gathered together at Pentecost in Jerusalem. Remember that the same Holy Spirit who filled their minds and hearts also fills the whole Church today. And He brings us the loveliest and the most powerful gifts: "love, joy, peace, patience, kindness, goodness, trustfulness, gentleness and self-control" (Gal. 5:22).

Let us really accept the words of Jesus: "If anyone thirst, let him come to me and drink" (Jn. 7:37). Then we shall receive His gift: "Out of our hearts shall flow rivers of living water.... Now he said this about the

Spirit, which those who believed in him were to receive." Then, in the power of the Spirit we shall become a people that prays: indeed, the Spirit Himself will pray in us and for us (cf. Rom. 8:26). And we shall become a holy people.

My dear brothers and sisters in Christ, realize the greatness of your Christian vocation. Christ has called you out of darkness into His own wonderful light. Consider what God has done for you in Baptism, and lift up your eyes and see the final glory that awaits you.

"Bless the Lord, O my soul.

O Lord my God, you are very great.

O Lord how manifold are all your works.

When you send forth your Spirit, they are created, and you renew the face of the earth" (Ps. 104:1, 24, 30). Amen.

Common Declaration of John Paul II and the Archbishop of Canterbury

The following is the text of the Common Declaration of John Paul II and Dr. Runcie, Archbishop of Canterbury, which was read in Canterbury Cathedral on the eve of Pentecost.

1. In the Cathedral Church of Christ at Canterbury the Pope and the Archbishop of Canterbury have met on the eve of Pentecost to offer thanks to God for the progress that has been made in the work of reconciliation between our communions. Together with leaders of other Christian Churches and communities we have listened to the Word of God; together we have recalled our one Baptism and renewed the promises then made; together we have acknowledged the witness given by those whose faith has led them to surrender the precious gift of life itself in the service of others, both in the past and in modern times.

2. The bond of our common Baptism into Christ led our Predecessors to inaugurate a serious dialogue between our Churches, a dialogue founded on the Gospels and the ancient common traditions, a dialogue which has as its goal the unity for which Christ prayed to His Father "so that the world may know that you have sent me and have loved them even

as you have loved me" (Jn. 17:23). In 1966, our Predecessors Pope Paul VI and Archbishop Michael Ramsey made a Common Declaration announcing their intention to inaugurate a serious dialogue between the Roman Catholic Church and the Anglican Communion which would "include not only theological matters such as Scripture, Tradition and liturgy, but also matters of practical difficulty felt on either side" (Common Declaration, par. 6). After this dialogue had already produced three statements on Eucharist, ministry and ordination, and authority in the Church, Pope Paul VI and Archbishop Donald Coggan, in their Common Declaration in 1977, took the occasion to encourage the completion of the dialogue on these three important questions so that the commission's conclusions might be evaluated by the respective authorities through procedures appropriate to each communion. The Anglican-Roman Catholic International Commission has now completed the task assigned to it with the publication of its final report, and as our two communions proceed with the necessary evaluation, we join in thanking the members of the commission for their dedication, scholarship and integrity in a long and demanding task undertaken for love of Christ and for the unity of His Church.

3. The completion of this commission's work bids us look to the next stage of our common pilgrimage in faith and hope towards the unity for which we long. We are agreed that it is now time to set up a new international Commission. Its task will be to continue the work already begun: to examine, especially in the light of our respective judgments on the final report, the outstanding doctrinal differ-

ences which still separate us, with a view towards their eventual resolution; to study all that hinders the mutual recognition of the ministries of our communions; and to recommend what practical steps will be necessary when, on the basis of our unity in faith, we are able to proceed to the restoration of full communion. We are well aware that this new commission's task will not be easy, but we are encouraged by our reliance on the grace of God and by all that we have seen of the power of that grace in the ecumenical movement of our time.

4. While this necessary work of theological clarification continues, it must be accompanied by the zealous work and fervent prayer of Roman Catholics and Anglicans throughout the world as they seek to grow in mutual understanding, fraternal love and common witness to the Gospel. Once more then, we call on the bishops, clergy and faithful people of both our communions in every country, diocese and parish in which our faithful live side by side. We urge them all to pray for this work and to adopt every possible means of furthering it through their collaboration in deepening their allegiance to Christ and in witnessing to Him before the world. Only by such collaboration and prayer can the memory of the past enmities be healed and our past antagonisms overcome.

5. Our aim is not limited to the union of our two communions alone, to the exclusion of other Christians, but rather extends to the fulfillment of God's will for the visible unity of all His people. Both in our present dialogue, and in those engaged in by other Christians among themselves and with us, we recognize in the agreements we are able to reach, as well as

in the difficulties which we encounter, a renewed challenge to abandon ourselves completely to the truth of the Gospel. Hence we are happy to make this declaration today in the welcome presence of so many fellow Christians whose Churches and communities are already partners with us in prayer and work for the unity of all.

6. With them we wish to serve the cause of peace, of human freedom and human dignity, so that God may indeed be glorified in all His creatures. With them we greet in the name of God all men of good will, both those who believe in Him and those who are still searching for Him.

7. This holy place reminds us of the vision of Pope Gregory in sending St. Augustine as an apostle to England, full of zeal for the preaching of the Gospel and the shepherding of the flock. On this eve of Pentecost, we turn again in prayer to Jesus, the Good Shepherd, who promised to ask the Father to give us another Advocate to be with us forever, the Spirit of truth (cf. Jn. 14:16), to lead us to the full unity to which He calls us. Confident in the power of this same Holy Spirit, we commit ourselves anew to the task of working for unity with firm faith, renewed hope and ever deeper love.

Modern Warfare—Totally Unacceptable

On the feast of Pentecost, May 30, Pope John Paul celebrated Mass at Bagington Airport in Coventry and administered the Sacrament of Confirmation to 26 persons. To the very large crowd present for the occasion, Pope John Paul delivered the following address.

My dear brothers and sisters in Jesus Christ,

1. Peace be with you. On this great feast of Pentecost, I greet all of you who have come from so many parishes in the Province of Birmingham and beyond. I also greet our beloved brothers and sisters from other Christian Churches and ecclesial communities, whose presence bears witness to our one Baptism in Jesus Christ and to our openness to the one Holy Spirit. And so my first words to you all are: "Peace be with you."

We are close to the city of Coventry, a city devastated by war but rebuilt in hope. The ruins of the old cathedral and the building of the new are recognized throughout the world as a symbol of Christian reconciliation and peace. We pray at this Mass: "Send forth your Spirit, O Lord, and renew the face of the earth." In this prayer we call upon God to enable us to bring about that reconciliation and peace not simply in symbol, but in reality too.

2. Our world is disfigured by war and violence. The ruins of the old cathedral constantly remind our society of its capacity to destroy. And today that capacity is greater than ever. People are having to live under the shadow of a nuclear nightmare. Yet people everywhere long for peace. Men and women of good will desire to make common cause in their search for a world-wide community of brotherhood and understanding. They long for justice, yes, but for justice filled with mercy. Being so close as we are to Shakespeare's birthplace we would do well to consider this: "that in the course of justice none of us should see salvation. We do pray for mercy and that same prayer does teach all of us to render the deeds of mercy."

What is this peace for which we long? What is this peace symbolized by the new Cathedral of Coventry? Peace is not just the absence of war. It involves mutual respect and confidence between peoples and nations. It involves collaboration and binding agreements. *Like a cathedral, peace has to be constructed,* patiently and with unshakeable faith.

Wherever the strong exploit the weak; wherever the rich take advantage of the poor; wherever great powers seek to dominate and to impose ideologies, there the work of making peace is undone; there the cathedral of peace is again destroyed. Today, the scale and the horror of modern warfare—whether nuclear or not—makes it totally unacceptable as a means of settling differences between nations. War should belong to the tragic past, to history; it should find no place on humanity's agenda for the future.

And so, this morning, I invite you to pray with me for the cause of peace. Let us pray earnestly for the special session of the United Nations on Disarmament which begins soon. The voices of Christians join with others in urging the leaders of the world to abandon confrontation and to turn their backs on policies which require the nations to spend vast sums of money for weapons of mass destruction. We pray this Pentecost that the Holy Spirit may inspire the leaders of the world to engage in fruitful dialogue. May the Holy Spirit lead them to adopt peaceful ways of safeguarding liberty which do not involve the threat of nuclear disaster.

Yet the cathedral of peace is built of many small stones. Each person has to become a stone in that beautiful edifice. All people must deliberately and resolutely commit themselves to the pursuit of peace. Mistrust and division between nations begin in the heart of individuals. Work for peace starts when we listen to the urgent call of Christ: "Repent and believe in the gospel" (Mk. 1:15). We must turn from domination to service; we must turn from violence to peace; we must turn from ourselves to Christ, who alone can give us a new heart, a new understanding. Each individual, at some moment in his or her life, is destined to hear this call from Christ. Each person's response leads to death or to life. Faith in Christ, the Incarnate Word of God, will bring us into the way of peace.

YOU WILL WITNESS TO THE TRUTH OF THE GOSPEL

3. I would now like to speak especially to the young people who are about to receive the Sacrament of Confirmation. Today's Gospel has special meaning

for you, for it says that "Jesus came and stood among them. He said to them, 'Peace be with you,' and showed them his hands and his side. The disciples were filled with joy when they saw the Lord, and he said to them again, 'Peace be with you. As the Father sent me, so I am sending you.' After saying this he breathed on them and said: 'Receive the Holy Spirit'" (Jn. 20:20-22).

Christ's gift of the Holy Spirit is going to be poured out upon you in a particular way. You will hear the words of the Church spoken over you, calling upon the Holy Spirit to confirm your faith, to seal you in His love, to strengthen you for His service. You will then take your place among fellow Christians throughout the world, full citizens now of the People of God. You will witness to the truth of the Gospel in the name of Jesus Christ. You will live your lives in such a way as to make holy all human life. Together with all the confirmed, you will become living stones in the cathedral of peace. Indeed you are called by God to be instruments of His peace.

ONE BODY, ONE PEOPLE, ONE CHURCH

4. Today you must understand that you are not alone. We are one body, one people, one Church of Christ. The sponsor who stands at your side represents for you the whole community. Together with a great crowd of witnesses drawn from all peoples and every age, you represent Christ. *You* are young people who *have received a mission from Christ,* for He says to you today: "As the Father sent me, so I am sending you."

Let me recall for a moment the memory of two great Englishmen who can inspire you today. Study the example of St. Boniface, born at Crediton in Devon, one of your greatest fellow countrymen and also one of the Church's greatest missionaries. And the Holy Spirit, given to Boniface through the Sacraments of Baptism and Confirmation, strengthened his personal love for Christ and brought him to a maturity of faith. This faith radiated through his whole life. He longed to share it with others, even with those in other lands. And so, with complete trust in God and with courage and perseverance, he helped to establish the Church on the continent of Europe. You, too, must show courage and perseverance in living by the standards of the Gospel in all the circumstances of your lives.

I cannot come to the Midlands without remembering that great man of God, that pilgrim for truth, Cardinal John Henry Newman. His quest for God and for the fullness of truth—a sign of the Holy Spirit at work within him—brought him to a prayerfulness and a wisdom which still inspire us today. Indeed Cardinal Newman's many years of seeking a fuller understanding of the Faith reflect his abiding confidence in the words of Christ: "I shall ask the Father and he will give you another Advocate to be with you for ever, that Spirit of truth whom the world can never receive since it neither sees nor knows him" (Jn. 14:16-17). And so I commend to you his example of persevering faith and longing for the truth. He can help you to draw nearer to God, in whose presence he lived, and to whose service he gave himself totally. His teaching has great importance today in our search for Christian unity too, not only in this country but throughout the world. Imitate his humility and his obedience to God; pray for a wisdom like his, a wisdom that can come from God alone.

POWER TO THE APOSTLES

5. "Jesus breathed on them and said: 'Receive the Holy Spirit. For those whose sins you forgive, they are forgiven; for those whose sins you retain, they are retained.'"

On that first Pentecost our Savior gave the Apostles the power to forgive sins when He poured into their hearts the gift of the Holy Spirit. The same Holy Spirit comes to you today in the Sacrament of Confirmation to involve you more completely in the Church's fight against sin and in her mission of fostering holiness. He comes to dwell more fully in your hearts and to strengthen you for the struggle with evil. My dear young people, the world of today needs you, for it needs men and women who are filled with the Holy Spirit. It needs your courage and hopefulness, your faith and your perseverance. The world of tomorrow will be built by you. Today you receive the gift of the Holy Spirit so that you may work with deep faith and with abiding charity, so that you may help to bring to the world the fruits of reconciliation and peace. Strengthened by the Holy Spirit and His manifold gifts, commit yourselves wholeheartedly to the Church's struggle against sin. Strive to be unselfish; try not to be obsessed with material things. Be active members of the People of God; be reconciled with each other and devoted to the work of justice, which will bring peace on earth.

OPEN TO HIS GIFTS

6. "How many are your works, O Lord!" (Ps. 104:24)

These words of the responsorial psalm evoke gratitude from our hearts and a hymn of praise from our lips. Indeed how many are the works of the Lord, how great are the effects of the Holy Spirit's action in Confirmation! When this sacrament is conferred, the words of the psalm are fulfilled among us: "You send forth your spirit, they are created; and you renew the face of the earth" (v. 30).

On the first day of Pentecost the Holy Spirit came upon the Apostles and upon Mary and filled them with His power. Today we remember that moment and we open ourselves again to the gift of that same Holy Spirit. In that Spirit we are baptized. In that Spirit we are confirmed. In that Spirit we are called to share in the mission of Christ. In that Spirit we shall indeed become the people of Pentecost, the apostles of our time. "Come, O Holy Spirit, fill the hearts of your faithful and kindle in them the fire of your love." Amen.

May the Generosity of Your Hearts Never Weaken

In the afternoon of May 30, Pope John Paul went to Liverpool. During the ceremony at Speke Airport, ten kilometers from the city, the Holy Father replied to Archbishop Worlock's address of welcome as follows.

My brothers and sisters in Jesus Christ,

1. Thank you for your kind welcome. Thank you for coming here to greet me. In my turn, I greet you in the words of the risen Savior: Peace be with you. May peace be in your homes, and may the peace of Christ reign in your minds and hearts.

It is good to be here. I am glad to pay my first visit to this region of England and to the city of Liverpool of which you are so proud.

Here near to the sea, I am reminded that you are a seafaring nation. For centuries the people of these islands have traded by sea, explored by sea and made a living from the sea. I am also thinking of the many missionaries—priests, sisters, brothers and lay people—who have sailed from your ports to play their part in building up the life of the Church in other lands. These men and women are a sign of the vitality of the faith which you have received and cherished. And their going forth upon the sea is a symbol of the confidence and trust which Christ asks of all His disciples.

MAY THE GENEROSITY OF YOUR HEARTS NEVER WEAKEN

We do well, too, to remember in our prayers those who have given their lives at sea and whose resting place bears no stone or monument. May they rest in the peace of the Lord. For so long your city of Liverpool has been a great port. People of many lands have made it their home. Here in past centuries people have seen the face of suffering, caused by such evils as slavery and great poverty. You have also witnessed the achievements of technical progress and human development. But perhaps your greatest heritage is found in all those who have struggled here to overcome the ills of society and to build up a common brotherhood. In this regard I am told that you have your own pioneer of charity, Fr. Nugent.

2. It is only fitting that I should take this occasion to acknowledge the generosity for which Britain has long been known. Though the links between this nation and other parts of the world have changed in the course of time, much aid is still sent to those in need, especially in the developing countries—and lately to my own homeland. I remember how Cardinal Heenan, who had once been Archbishop of Liverpool, told the Polish bishops during the Second Vatican Council: "It was the Polish pilots who saved England during the war." His words and your recent assistance to Poland show the strong ties of concern and friendship which have existed for years between Poland and Britain. I pray that these ties will be ever deepened and renewed.

I hope that, despite all obstacles, the generosity of your hearts will never weaken. I hope that, through programs such as the Catholic Fund for Overseas Development, you will continue to help the poor, to feed the hungry and to contribute to the cause of development. Always keep alive your Gospel tradition of loving concern and service to others in the name of Jesus.

3. Our times present us with many challenges and difficulties. One problem in particular which I would like to mention is *unemployment*. I know that you are experiencing this very seriously in Liverpool, and it is one of the major problems facing society as a whole. In many countries, unemployment has risen sharply and caused hardship to individuals and families. It tends to sow seeds of bitterness, division and even violence. The young, unable to find a job, feel cheated of their dreams, while those who have lost their jobs feel rejected and useless. This tragedy affects every aspect of life, from the material and physical to the mental and spiritual. It therefore very much concerns the Church, which makes her own the hardships and sufferings, as well as the joys and hopes, of the men and women of our time. It is a matter of vital importance and it deserves the attention and prayers of all people of good will.

4. I greet warmly all the disabled who have come here to meet me today. You have a special place in my heart and in the love of Christ. And I assure you that your role in the Church is a most important one. You and those who are sick and infirm build up the kingdom of God when you patiently accept your sufferings and offer them with Christ as a pleasing sacrifice to our heavenly Father. As St. Paul said, your sufferings help ''to make up all that has still to be undergone by Christ for the sake of his body, the Church'' (Col. 1:24).

I have been told that as I travel through Liverpool our motorcade will be passing along Hope Street. This name struck me immediately as an expression of the aspirations of the people who live here, an expression of their hope for the future, especially for the future of their children and their children's children. So many dangers and problems face our young people today. I have already mentioned unemployment. In addition there are such evils as alcoholism and drug addiction, pornography, misguided notions of sexuality, and increasing crime and violence.

All these ills of society could bring us to disillusionment and even despair, if we were not a people of hope, if we did not have a deep and abiding confidence in the power and mercy of God. And so our young people, indeed all of us, need the virtue of hope, a hope founded not on fantasy and dreams, not even on what is seen, but a hope which arises from our faith in the God who loves us and is our gentle and merciful Father. "Glory be to him whose power, working in us, can do infinitely more than we can ask or imagine; glory be to him from generation to generation in the Church and in Christ Jesus for ever and ever. Amen" (Eph. 3:20-21).

The Church Continues Christ's Work of Reconciliation

On May 30, a concelebrated Mass in the Metropolitan Cathedral of Christ the King in Liverpool was dedicated to the theme of penance and reconciliation. Pope John Paul delivered the following homily at the Mass.

Praised be Jesus Christ.

1. As Pentecost Sunday draws to its close, we have come to this Church, the Cathedral Church of Christ the King, here in Liverpool, to celebrate the Holy Eucharist, the source and summit of Christian life and the sacrament of unity and love.

In my apostolic pilgrimage through Britain it is my joy not only to celebrate the Eucharist, but also to administer other sacraments to the faithful of the local Churches. I have already had the opportunity to baptize and confirm and to confer the Sacrament of the Anointing of the Sick. Although it is not possible this evening to celebrate the Sacrament of Penance, nevertheless I wish to emphasize *the importance of penance and reconciliation in the life of the Church* and in the lives of all her individual members.

Two years ago, the National Pastoral Congress gathered in this cathedral to begin its work with a service of repentance and reconciliation. Those present prayed for healing and mercy, and for the grace to be faithful to God's will. They asked for light and wisdom to guide their deliberations and to deepen their love for the Church. This evening we assemble around this same altar to give honor and glory to the Lord, to praise our God who is rich in mercy. We see the need for conversion and reconciliation. We too pray for understanding where there has been discord. We seek unity from the same Holy Spirit who grants various gifts to the faithful and different ministries to the Church.

A COMPLETELY FREE GIFT

2. Before the first Pentecost, Jesus said to His disciples: "Receive the Holy Spirit. For those whose sins you forgive, they are forgiven; for those whose sins you retain, they are retained" (Jn. 20:23). These words of our Savior remind us of the fundamental gift of our redemption: the gift of having our sins forgiven and of being reconciled with God. Remission of sin is a completely free and undeserved gift, a newness of life which we could never earn. God grants it to us out of His mercy. As St. Paul wrote: "It is all God's work. It was God who reconciled us to himself through Christ and gave us the work of handing on this reconciliation" (2 Cor. 5:18).

There is no sin which cannot be forgiven, if we approach the throne of mercy with humble and contrite hearts. No evil is more powerful than the infinite mercy of God. In becoming man, Jesus entered completely into our human experience, even to the point of suffering the final and most cruel effect of the power of sin—death on a cross. He really became one like us in all things but sin. But evil with all its power did not win. By dying, Christ destroyed our death; by rising, He restored our life; by His wounds we are healed and our sins are forgiven. For this reason, when the Lord appeared to His disciples after the resurrection, He showed them His hands and His side. He wanted them to see that the victory had been won; to see that He, the risen Christ, had *transformed the marks of sin and death into symbols of hope and life.*

ALWAYS RECONCILING

3. By the victory of His cross, Jesus Christ won for us the forgiveness of our sins and reconciliation with God. And it is these gifts that Christ offers us when He gives the Holy Spirit to the Church, for He said to the Apostles: "Receive the Holy Spirit. For those whose sins you forgive, they are forgiven" (Jn. 20:23). Through the power of the Holy Spirit, the Church continues Christ's work of reconciling the world to Himself. In every age the Church remains the community of those who have been reconciled with God, the community of those who have received the reconciliation that was willed by God the Father and achieved through the sacrifice of His beloved Son.

The Church is also by her nature always reconciling, handing on to others the gift that she herself has received, the gift of having been forgiven and made one with God. She does this in many ways, but especially through the sacraments, and in particular through Penance. In this consoling sacrament she leads each of the faithful individually to Christ, and through the Church's ministry, Christ Himself gives forgiveness, strength and mercy. Through this highly personal sacrament, Christ continues to meet the men and women of our time. He restores wholeness where there was division, He communicates light where darkness reigned, and He gives a hope and joy which the world could never give. Through this sacrament the Church proclaims to the world the infinite riches of God's mercy, that mercy which has broken down barriers which divided us from God and from one another.

ROLE OF THE PRIEST

On this day of Pentecost, as the Church proclaims the reconciling action of Christ Jesus, and the power of His Holy Spirit, I appeal to all the faithful of Britain —and to all the other members of the Church who may hear my voice or read my words: Dearly beloved, let us give greater emphasis to the Sacrament of Penance in our own lives. Let us strive to safeguard what I described in my first encyclical as Christ's "right to meet each one of us in that key moment in the soul's life constituted by the moment of conversion and forgiveness" (RH 20). And in particular I ask you, my brother priests, to realize how closely and how effectively you can collaborate with the Saviôr in the divine work of reconciliation. For lack of time, certain worthy activities may have to be abandoned or postponed, but not the confessional. Always give priority to your specific priestly role in representing the Good Shepherd in the Sacrament of Penance. And as you witness and praise the marvelous action of the Holy Spirit in human hearts, you will feel yourselves called to further conversion and to deeper love of Christ and His flock.

BE FULLY RECONCILED

4. As Christians today strive to be sources of reconciliation in the world, they feel the need, perhaps more urgently than ever before, to be fully reconciled among themselves. *For the sin of disunity among Christians,* which has been with us for centuries, *weighs heavily upon the Church.* The seriousness of this sin was clearly shown at the Second Vatican Council, which stated: "Without doubt, this discord openly contradicts the will of Christ, provides a stumbling block to the world, and inflicts damage on the most holy cause of proclaiming the Good News to every creature" (UR 1).

Restoration of unity among Christians is one of the main concerns of the Church in the last part of the twentieth century. And this task is for all of us. No one can claim exemption from this responsibility. Indeed everyone can make some contribution, however small it may seem, and all are called to that interior conversion which is the essential condition for ecumenism. As the Second Vatican Council taught: "This change of heart and holiness of life, along with the public and private prayer for the unity of Christians, should be regarded as the soul of the whole ecumenical movement, and can rightly be called 'spiritual ecumenism' " *(ibid.,* no. 8).

The Holy Spirit, who is the source of all unity, provides the Body of Christ with a "variety of gifts" (1 Cor. 12:3), so that it may be built up and strengthened. As the Holy Spirit granted the Apostles the gift of tongues, so that all gathered in Jerusalem on that first Pentecost might hear and understand the one Gospel of Christ, should we not expect the same Holy

Spirit to grant us the gifts we need in order to continue the work of salvation, and to be reunited as one body in Christ? In this we trust and for this we pray, confident in the power which the Spirit gave to the Church at Pentecost.

5. "Send forth your Spirit...and renew the face of the earth" (Ps. 104:30). These words of the psalmist are our heartfelt prayer today, as we ask Almighty God to renew the face of the earth through the life-giving power of the Spirit. Send forth Your Spirit, O Lord, renew our hearts and minds with the gifts of light and truth. Renew our homes and families with the gifts of unity and joy. Renew our cities and our countries with true justice and lasting peace. Renew Your Church on earth with the gifts of penance and reconciliation, with unity in faith and love.

Send forth Your Spirit, O Lord, and renew the face of the earth!

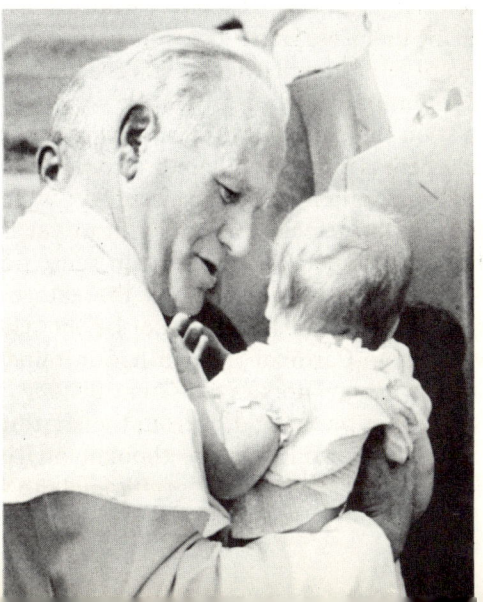

Historical Witness of Polish Emigration

In the Crystal Palace Sports Center of London, Pope John Paul met a large group of Polish people resident in Britain. He spoke to them in Polish, a translation of which follows.

Dear brothers and sisters, beloved fellow countrymen!

1. With wonderful force there were imprinted in my memory the words that Cardinal Heenan, Primate of England, said when during the Council he visited the Polish bishops staying at the college on the Aventine. He began his discourse with these words: "Polish aviators saved Great Britain!"

I refer to these words today because it seems to me that in them we must look for an answer to the question of your identity here. Who are you? Are you only a community of emigrants, like so many others that exist on the entire earth? Certainly yes. And it is certainly necessary to seek here the comparison with the great emigration of the last century, which was concentrated principally in France. And yet there is something particular that in a certain sense does not allow you to be thought of with the categories of "emigration"; at least those cannot be thought of in this way whom Cardinal Heenan had in mind when he said: "Polish aviators saved Great Britain!"

You cannot be thought of from the starting point of "emigration"; you must be thought of from the starting point of the reality of "homeland." It is true that before the Second World War there was in England a certain number of Polish emigrants. However, those who were found here in the framework of the events of the war were not emigrants. They were Poland wrenched away from its own borders, from its own battlefields; Poland awakened, scarcely twenty years before its independent existence; Poland that was quickly rebuilding itself after the destructions and lesions of centuries; Poland, finally, that they yet again tried to divide, as in the eighteenth century, imposing upon it a horrible homicidal war, with the ruling forces of the invaders.

And so, what today we are accustomed to calling "English Poland" takes shape as the very marrow of the Poland that is fighting for the holy cause of its independence. The aviators that defended the British Isles made up this Poland; the divisions and companies fighting near Narvik; the divisions and companies that from the heart of the Soviet Republics of Western Europe and Asia; and then through Persia, the Middle East, Egypt and Libya, arrived on the Apennine Peninsula at Monte Cassino, contributing to the restoration of freedom to the "Italian land." I still have before my eyes that inscription posted along the street in Bologna that leads from the military cemetery to the center of the city (I traveled it on April 18 of this year). The inscription read: "Along this street your fellow countrymen entered, bringing us freedom—along the same street you bring us faith."

2. What I am saying flows from the living sense of history. You who have created today's "English Poland" are for me in the first place not emigration, but primarily the living part of Poland which, though

far from its native soil, does not cease being itself. Even more, it lives with the conviction that in it, in this very part, it lives as a whole in a particular way.

If I have found myself on English soil as a pilgrim, a pilgrim Pope, and at the same time as a son of your land, I cannot but express first of all this truth about you: the truth that I have always felt. I have felt its fundamental authenticity and at the same time its profound tragedy.

3. In fact, one cannot, reminding you of the irrevocable right to be (from the beginning) a singular part of Poland: government, army, administration, power structures throughout the country and outside of it, one cannot, I say, especially with the passing of years, one cannot help encountering this painful physical "absence" in which your lively and splendid, irremovable historical presence in Poland had to be changed...outside of Poland. One cannot help recalling, once again, that great emigration and those great, great spirits who, led by the sense of a live presence, directed a prayer to the absent homeland: "My homeland, you are like health: to completely appreciate you, one needs only to have lost you! Today your beauty in all its splendor I see and describe because in exile I pine for you!" (trans. of Clotilde Garosci—Pan Tadeusz—Torino 1955, second edition)

A mystery, in some way wonderful, of consciences and hearts began in the last century and returns to be repeated in the present century. Poland is one of the most tried countries in the whole world. One of the homelands most deeply furrowed by suffering, and at the same time one of the most loved.

Perhaps to the mystery of this unusual love for the homeland we can compare that wonderful spiritual displacement: through so many of its sons and daughters, and often through the best of them, it is spiritually present through physical absence. And then, for those who live in Poland, this absence is not only absence. It is a challenge. The "absent" not only "are not right"; at the same time they render an historical testimony. They speak of what was its true worth, and what remains its true worth.

Therefore your sacrifice and your toil, the blood of so many of our brothers and sisters, even though not achieving the objectives for which they fought, have not been useless.

History, above all, the history of our country, is full of noble deeds. We see them also in modern times. We know that efforts aimed at freedom, respect for the dignity of man, respect for his work, for the possibility of a life in peace with one's conscience and convictions, apparently have not achieved the intended results. However, they have changed the soul of the nation, its awareness. These efforts comfort the soul. They point out that in life there are other values, spiritual and moral, that are not measured by material worth, but are decisive values in the proper hierarchy of human existence.

4. Where does this interior strength of the Polish emigration spring from? We must look for its source at the Vistula, in the faith of the Poles and in their culture. It is, as I said in Gniezno during my pilgrimage to our homeland, "the expression of man.... Man creates it, and through it man creates himself...and at the same time he creates the culture in union with

others...the Polish culture is a good on which is based the spiritual life of the Poles. It distinguishes us as a nation. It determines us along the whole course of history, it determines much more than material strength does. And even still more than political frontiers. We know that the Polish nation has passed through the hard trial of the loss of independence for more than a hundred years, and in the midst of this trial it has always remained itself. It has remained spiritually independent because it has had its own culture. Further yet, in the periods of the partitions it has so much enriched and deepened it, because only through creating culture can it be preserved."

Today we must say that such was the case also after the Second World War. Well known are the merits of your emigration in the field of research and publications concerning the history of Poland, particularly its history in the last century. It is a great contribution to the awareness of the true history of the nations. If this contribution of research and publications were lacking, knowledge of the past of the national history would not be complete.

5. I also said at Gniezno that Polish culture bears clear Christian characteristics, and it is not by chance that the first literary monument that attests to this is the hymn *Bugurodzica* (Mother of God).

It is precisely to these Christian roots that we must always return and from them grow again in every era, because this is the truth about man. He must always discover it anew.

Emigration will achieve its mission more effectively the higher its ethical value is, the more Christ is the center of its life and activity, the more it believes that only He is "the way, the truth and the life" (Jn. 14:6).

In the Encyclical *Redemptor hominis* I wrote that "Jesus Christ meets the man of every age, including our own, with the same words: 'You will know the truth, and the truth will make you free....' Today also, even after two thousand years, we see Christ as the One who brings man freedom based on truth..." (no. 12).

We must say that you have understood and continue to understand the need for the bond with faith and with the Church. And therefore this emigration, as part of the nation, contained all the levels of the whole social profile, with the political, cultural, scientific, professional institutions, but also with the whole ecclesiastical organization. From the very first moment, the Church was present with all her structures. There was the bishop, the unforgettable Archbishop Joseph Gawlina, and later the rector of the Polish mission in England. There were priests and the religious organizations that developed. These centers were among the first organized. Thanks to the understanding and good will of the local hierarchy, but above all, thanks to your generosity and the sacrifice-laden work of the priests, there arose so many Polish chapels and churches that serve to strengthen the bonds with Christ and introduce you into the divine mysteries, uniting you with Him. Near the pastoral centers there were organized schools of the Polish language.

6. The bond with Polish culture is realized in the family home, in religious life, and in the life of the

organizations. On the other hand, the school, higher studies, and professional life, unite with the culture of the country of sojourn. The bond between the country of your forefathers and the country of sojourn is realized precisely at the level of culture. It offers a proper perspective of the society and through education prepares a young person for duties in the sphere of emigration and also for assuming the adequate attitude in life.

Therefore, one of the most important tasks is the passing on of the proper ideas to the new generations. Emigration must be fit for an adequate education of the total man. Only in this case will the younger generation be able to take up the idea of freedom and truth from the generation that is at its sunset.

The education of the total man—the education to truth and the education in the Christian and Polish tradition—begins in the family. The present state of public morality does not always assure the family, especially the parents, the necessary authority that belongs to them.

The causes that contribute to this are various. The family therefore is in need of a special pastoral care. Only the family, strong in God, aware of its Christian duties, can be in a position to fulfill the duties of the education of the total man, since, as I said on another occasion, "the work of the education of man is carried out not only with the help of institutions, with the help of organized material means, however excellent they may be...the most important thing is always man, man and his moral authority, which arises from the truth of his principles and from the conformity of his actions with these principles" (Address to UNESCO, June 2, 1980, no. 11).

A. MARI

On the first day of his visit to Great Britain, Pope John Paul II met with Queen Elizabeth II in Buckingham Palace.

A. MARI

Britain's Prince Charles had a meeting with the Holy Father in Canterbury.

A. MARI

The Holy Father was greeted by Church officials outside Canterbury Cathedral.

A. MARI

Pope John Paul II and Dr. Robert Runcie, Archbishop of Canterbury, recited the Lord's Prayer together in Canterbury Cathedral.

A. MARI

His Holiness and the Archbishop of Canterbury exchanged a sign of peace.

A. MARI

Pope John Paul II with the Choir of Canterbury Cathedral.

A. MARI

The Holy Father celebrated Mass for 100,000 people at Wembly Stadium.

A. MARI

Thirty bishops concelebrated the Mass with His Holiness.

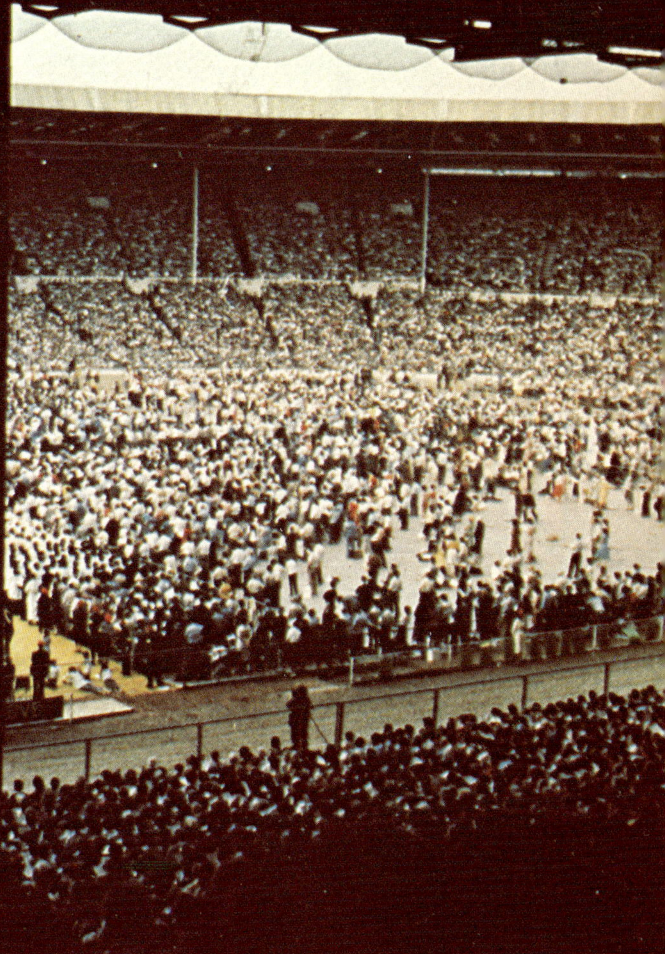

A. MARI

The last blessing of the Mass in Wembly Stadium.

A. MARI

At Gatwick Airport, London, children presented the Holy Father with flowers.

A. MARI

At Ninian Park in Cardiff, the Holy Father met a large group of young people from England and Wales.

A. MARI

A meeting with the handicapped in Edinburgh.

A. MARI

The Holy Father was welcomed by residents of St. Joseph's Hospital of Rosewell in Edinburgh.

A. MARI

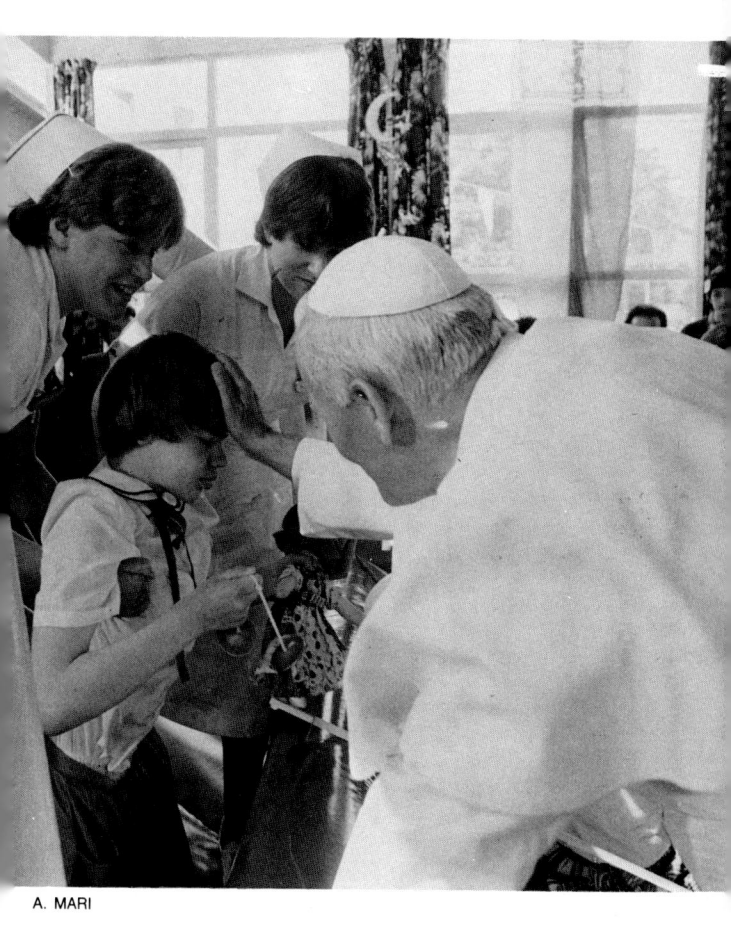

The Pope paid a brief visit to patients inside the hospital.

A. MARI

As everywhere, the Holy Father expressed his great love for children.

Today, therefore, I raise my voice from this place in the words of the Apostolic Exhortation *Familiaris consortio:* "Family, discover within yourself this summons that cannot be ignored! Family, 'become' what 'you are'! Called together by word and sacrament as the Church of the home, become both teacher and mother, the same as the worldwide Church" (cf. nos. 17, 38).

7. You wished today's meeting of ours to coincide with your main pilgrimage on the occasion of the six hundredth anniversary of the presence of the Mother of God, in her miraculous image, in Jasna Gora. We know what this sanctuary was and what it is, this effigy of Jasna Gora for the Polish nation.

Uniting myself to this common intention of yours, which is also mine, permit me to recall to our memory that great person, the late Primate of Poland, Cardinal Stefan Wyszynski. I do this at our gathering on the first anniversary of his death and his funeral, his passing from this earthly homeland, which he so unbendingly served, to the Father's house.

I do this at today's gathering with that same love with which all the Poles in our homeland and abroad surrounded him, looking at him as a providential man, given to the homeland during times of difficult choices and during the time of the new way. I see in him, as all of you, the man bound from the very depths of his soul with the mystery of the Mother of Jasna Gora present in the life of her children and in the life of our nation.

Those who left the country, in search of food or for other reasons, brought with them the image of Jasna Gora, or of Ostrobrama. It was an external sign of their faith and of their attachment to Christ and to Poland. The first emigrants in this country, those of the last century, brought the image of the Mother of God of Czestochowa to Manchester, as they did also to London. When Cardinal Augustus Hlond blessed the first Church in Devon, he dedicated it to the Mother of God of Czestochowa.

This image, during the last war, was in almost all the chapels of the military camps, and the same little images were often found in the divisions of Polish soldiers. The images of Our Lady of Czestochowa are found in every church where you gather for prayer, particularly to assist at Sunday Mass. It is in almost every home of the emigrants.

The jubilee year is the year of particular renewal of faith, of family life. It is necessary for parents, looking at Mary, to make themselves aware once more of their responsibilities and educational duties. To be sure, many families recite the prayer of Jasna Gora: "Mary, Queen of Poland, I am near you, I remember you, I keep watch." Let us be near her and let us keep watch! May the elderly be near her and keep watch! May the young keep watch. I address you particularly, my dear young friends. Have the courage to take up this difficult heritage and to develop it. There are so many problems today, so many values that demand that we keep watch lest man erase within himself, in his ties and social relations, the image and likeness of God inscribed in him by the Creator and renewed by Christ; may he not erase it in others!

8. It is not by chance that this unusual meeting of ours takes place on the Solemnity of Pentecost.

"Come, Holy Spirit,
send us a ray of your light from heaven."

Convince us of sin, of justice and of judgment (cf. Jn. 16:8).

Lead us to the whole truth (cf. Jn. 16:13).

Glorify Christ in us, take what is His and reveal it to us (cf. Jn. 16:14).

Remind us of all that Christ has told us (cf. Jn. 14:26).

Let not your hearts be disturbed, and do not fear (cf. Jn. 14:27).

In the Spirit of Vatican Council II

On May 31, the Holy Father traveled by helicopter from Speke Airport to Heaton Park, Manchester. On arrival he went to the convent of the Sisters of Nazareth where he met representatives of the Jewish community of England and spoke to them as follows:

I should first say that I followed your speech with great interest and I pondered the arguments you included in this speech. My answer is rather brief and not so full of arguments as your speech, but I am very grateful for your having put all these questions in your speech.

It is a joy for me to extend my fraternal greetings this morning to you, leading members of the Jewish Community. Particularly I greet the Chief Rabbi of the Commonwealth, Sir Emmanuel Yocobovich, together with other distinguished colleagues. On the occasion of my visit to Britain I wish to express my personal sentiments of esteem and friendship for all of you. At the same time I wish to reiterate the full respect of the Catholic Church for the Jewish people throughout the world. In the spirit of the Second Vatican Council, I recall the desire of the Church to collaborate willingly with you in the great cause of mankind, knowing that we have a common tradition that honors the sanctity of God and calls us to love the Lord our God with all our heart and with all our soul.

I extend cordial greetings to all those whom you represent.

Be Ambassadors of Christ and Win Back the World for God!

On the morning of May 31, the Holy Father concelebrated Mass in Heaton Park, Manchester, in the course of which he ordained twelve deacons to the priesthood and gave the following homily.

My brothers and sisters in Jesus Christ,

1. I greet you in the joy of the Holy Spirit! The coming of the Holy Spirit upon the Church is for every Christian a time of celebration and an opportunity for spiritual renewal. How pleased I am to be here in Manchester, to celebrate this great feast and to pray with you that the life-giving power of the Divine Paraclete will help the members of this Church to carry out their responsibilities as "a new creation."

To be a new creation is the vocation of all the baptized. St. Paul reminds us of this in the words of today's second reading: "...for anyone who is in Christ, there is a new creation; the old creation has gone, and now the new one is here" (2 Cor. 5:17). We must therefore give up the old order of the flesh, of sinfulness and living for ourselves. We must live "for him who died and was raised to life" for us (2 Cor. 5:15). Every believer is called to discipleship. By steadfastness in prayer, by compassion for those in need, by concern for justice in human affairs, Christians exercise the priesthood of the faithful, a living fellowship in Christ offering praise and glory to God our Father.

BE MEN OF GOD

2. But if we can apply the attributes of this new order of creation to the priesthood of the faithful, how much more compelling is their application to the ministerial or hierarchical priesthood, which is directed towards the sanctification of God's people.

3. My dear brothers, candidates for the priesthood: for you Christ today renews His prayer to the Father: "Consecrate them in truth, your word is truth" (Jn. 17:17). This consecration makes you even more a "new creation." It sets you apart from the world, so that you may be completely dedicated to God. It gives you the mission to act as Christ's ambassadors in reconciling the world to God. It was for this purpose that Jesus came from the Father and was born of the Virgin Mary. And it is this same mission which Christ entrusted to His disciples: "As you sent me into the world, I have sent them into the world, and for their sake I consecrate myself so that they too may be consecrated in truth" (Jn. 17:18).

At this important moment of your lives I say to you young men: realize how deeply Jesus desires you to be consecrated as He Himself is consecrated. Realize how closely the bond of priesthood joins you to Christ. Be worthy of the privilege you are going to receive of bringing God's gifts of love to His people and offering to God the people's prayerful response.

4. You must be men of God, His close friends. You must develop daily patterns of prayer, and penance

must be a regular part of your life. Prayer and penance will help you to appreciate more deeply that the strength of your ministry is found in the Lord and not in human resources.

England is fortunate to have a distinguished legacy of holy priests. Many of her sons left home and country in penal times to prepare for the priesthood. After ordination, they returned to England to face danger and often death for their faith. Manchester is rightly proud of its great martyr, St. Ambrose Barlow, the Benedictine. Catholic Lancashire honors its other martyrs: St. Edmund Arrowsmith and all those saints called "John": John Almond, John Plessington, John Rigby, John Southworth. But in addition to your martyrs, rejoice in the memory of many holy priests from this region who lived each day the fullness of their vocation. Near here, in Sutton, St. Helens, is the tomb of Blessed Dominic Barberi, the Passionist from Italy who received John Henry Newman into the Church. He is but one example of the countless other priests who continue to serve as models of holiness for the clergy of today.

5. You must try to deepen every day your friendship with Christ. You must also learn to share the hopes and the joys, the sorrows and the frustrations of the people entrusted to your care. Bring to them Christ's saving message of reconciliation. Visit your parishioners in their homes. This has been a strength of the Church in England. It is a pastoral practice that should not be neglected.

And do not forget all those with special needs, particularly those who are in prison, and their families. In the Gospel, Christ identifies Himself with prisoners when He says: "I was in prison and you visited me." And remember, that He did not specify whether they were innocent or guilty. Because you represent Christ, no one can be excluded from your pastoral love. I ask you, together with your brother priests, to take my greetings to all the prisons of Britain. Especially to the large one in Manchester. Through you, Jesus Christ wants to offer peace of conscience and the forgiveness of all sins. Through you, Jesus Christ wants to enkindle hope anew in their hearts. Through you, Jesus Christ wants to love those for whom He died. Teach all your people that you believe in that faithful love by the fidelity with which you live your own life. You must proclaim the Gospel with your life. When you celebrate the sacraments at the decisive moments of their lives, help them to trust in Christ's promised mercy and compassion. When you offer the redeeming Sacrifice of the Eucharist, help them to understand the need for transforming this great love into works of charity.

6. My brothers, be aware of the effect on others of the witness of lives. Your ordination is a source of consolation for those who have already given many years of priestly service, large numbers of whom are present today. The Lord is grateful for their labor and today He blesses them with the assurance that He will continue to provide for the future of the Church. May all these priests be renewed in the joyful enthusiasm of their early call, and may they continue to give generously of themselves in Christ's priestly work of reconciling the world to the Father.

I know of the many priests who could not be here because of old age or infirmity. To them also I send the expression of my love in Christ Jesus. Their prayers, their wisdom, their suffering are rich treasures for the Church, from which will come forth abundant blessings.

7. And what of your contemporaries? Undoubtedly your acceptance of Christ's mission is a clear witness for those who are not yet sure what the Lord wants of them. You show them that being ordained for God's service is a noble vocation that demands faith, courage and self-sacrifice. I am sure that such qualities are to be found among the young people of Great Britain. To them I say: be certain that Christ's call to the priesthood or religious life is addressed to some of you. Be certain that if you listen to His call and follow Him in the priesthood or religious life, you will find great joy and happiness. Be generous, take courage and remember His promise: "My yoke is easy and my burden light" (Mt. 11:30).

8. Finally, I wish to greet the parents and families of those about to be ordained. I say in the name of the Church, in the company of my fellow bishops, thank you for your generosity. It was you who brought these men into the world. It was you who first gave them the faith and the values that have helped to lead them to God's altar today. The Church, too, must be a family, bishops, priests, deacons, religious and laity, supporting each other and sharing with each other the individual gifts given by God. Every priest relies on the faith and talents of his parish community. If he is wise he will not only know the joy of dispensing God's grace, but also of receiving it abundantly through his parishioners as well. The partnership between priests and people is built upon prayer, col-

laboration and mutual respect and love. That has always been the tradition of these islands. May it never be lost.

9. Through this ordination the Lord really and truly continues the work of His "new creation." And He continues to send forth His message over all the earth and to speak personally to those who will be ordained: " 'Go now to those to whom I send you and say whatever I command you. Do not be afraid of them, for I am with you to protect you'—it is the Lord who speaks!" (Jer. 1:7-8) Amen.

Love in the Family Is a Guarantee for the Future of Humanity

In the afternoon of May 31, at York, the Holy Father met people from Northeast England. Tens of thousands participated in the Mass, the theme of which was matrimony, and during which there took place the renewal of marriage promises. In the course of the liturgy, Pope John Paul delivered the following homily.

My brothers and sisters,

1. On this feast of the Visitation of the Blessed Virgin Mary I greet you in the Lord. I am happy to be with you in this historic city of York. We are in the shadow, as it were, of the beautiful Minster, and in the spiritual company of so many saintly men and women who have graced these northern counties.

I deeply appreciate the presence here of many fellow Christians. I rejoice that we are united in a common Baptism and in our renewed search for full Christian unity.

I greet all those civic representatives from different cities and towns of Northern England. I thank you all for your welcome.

I am conscious of the history, especially the religious history, of this part of England. I refer to Holy Island where Aidan and Cuthbert brought the Catholic Faith. I recall Bede, who wrote so lovingly of the early life of the Church in England. I remember that a thousand years later men and women laid down their lives in this region for the Faith they loved. Mary Ward taught the Gospel of Jesus Christ to English exiles; Margaret Clitherow gave her life in this city of York. These holy women inspire women today to take their rightful place in the life of the Church, as befits their equality of rights and particular dignity. In that same period the priest, Nicholas Postgate, carried the Gospel across the moors and gave his life on this very spot.

This morning, in Manchester, young men were ordained to the sacred priesthood of Christ. They were answering the call of God's love. For many people, as for Margaret Clitherow, that call from God comes in and through marriage and family life. This is our theme. In our liturgical setting, which calls to mind the supremacy of God's saving grace, you married people will be invited to renew the promises you first made on your wedding day.

UNBREAKABLE ALLIANCE

2. In a marriage a man and a woman pledge themselves to one another in an unbreakable alliance of total mutual self-giving. A total union of love. Love that is not a passing emotion or temporary infatuation, but a responsible and free decision to bind oneself completely, "in good times and in bad," to one's partner. It is the gift of oneself to the other. It is a love to be proclaimed before the eyes of the whole world. It is unconditional.

To be capable of such love calls for careful preparation from early childhood to wedding day. It requires the constant support of Church and society throughout its development.

The love of husband and wife in God's plan leads beyond itself and new life is generated, a family is born. The family is a community of love and life, a home in which children are guided to maturity.

3. *Marriage is a holy sacrament.* Those baptized in the name of the Lord Jesus are married in His name also. Their love is a sharing in the love of God. He is its source. The marriages of Christian couples, today renewed and blessed, are images on earth of the wonder of God, the loving, life-giving communion of Three Persons in one God, and of God's covenant in Christ, with the Church.

Christian marriage is a sacrament of salvation. It is the pathway to holiness for all members of a family. With all my heart, therefore, I urge that your homes be centers of prayer; homes where families are at ease in the presence of God; homes to which others are invited to share hospitality, prayer and the praise of God: "With gratitude in your hearts sing psalms and hymns and inspired songs to God; and never say or do anything except in the name of the Lord Jesus Christ, giving thanks to God the Father through him" (Col. 3:16, 17).

In your country, there are many marriages between Catholics and other baptized Christians. Sometimes these couples experience special difficulties. To these families I say: you live in your marriage the hopes and difficulties of the path to Christian unity. Express that hope in prayer together, in the unity of love. Together invite the Holy Spirit of love into your hearts and into your homes. He will help you to grow in trust and understanding.

POSITIVE ASPECTS

4. Brothers and sisters, "May the peace of Christ reign in your hearts...let the message of Christ, in all its richness, find a home with you" (Col. 3:15, 16).

Recently I wrote an Apostolic Exhortation to the whole Catholic Church regarding the role of the Christian Family in the modern world. In that exhortation I underlined the positive aspects of family life today, which include: a more lively awareness of personal freedom and greater attention to the quality of interpersonal relationships in marriage, greater attention to promoting the dignity of women, to responsible procreation, to the education of children. But at the same time I could not fail to draw attention to the negative phenomena: a corruption of the idea and experience of freedom, with consequent self-centeredness in human relations; serious misconceptions regarding the relationship between parents and children; the growing number of divorces; the scourge of abortion; the spread of a contraceptive and anti-life mentality. Besides these destructive forces, there are social and economic conditions which affect millions of human beings, undermining the strength and stability of marriage and family life. In addition there is the cultural onslaught against the family by those who attack married life as "irrelevant" and "outdated." All of this is a serious challenge to society and to the Church. As I wrote then: "History is not simply a fixed progression towards what is better, but rather an event of freedom, and even a struggle between freedoms that are in mutual conflict" (FC 6).

Married couples, I speak to you of the hopes and ideals that sustain the Christian vision of marriage and family life. You will find the strength to be faithful to your marriage vows in your love for God and in your love for each other and for your children. Let this love be the rock that stands firm in the face of every storm and temptation. What better blessing could the Pope wish for your families than what Saint Paul wished for the Christians of Colossae: "Be clothed in sincere compassion, in kindness and humility, gentleness and patience. Bear with one another; forgive each other as soon as a quarrel begins. The Lord has forgiven you; now you must do the same. Over all these...put on love" (Col. 3:12-14).

BRIDGES ARE MEANT TO BE BUILT, NOT BROKEN

5.. Being a parent today brings worries and difficulties, as well as joys and satisfactions. Your children are your treasure. They love you very much, even if they sometimes find it hard to express that love. They look for independence and are reluctant to conform. Sometimes they wish to reject past traditions and even reject their faith.

In the family, bridges are meant to be built, not broken; and new expressions of wisdom and truth can be fashioned from the meeting of experience and enquiry. Yours is a true and proper ministry in the Church. Open the doors of your home and of your heart to all the generations of your family.

6. We cannot overlook the fact that some marriages fail. But still it is our duty to proclaim the true plan of God for all married love and to insist on fidel-

ity to that plan, as we go towards the fullness of life in the kingdom of heaven. Let us not forget that God's love for His people, Christ's love for the Church, is everlasting and can never be broken. And the covenant between a man and a woman joined in Christian marriage is as indissoluble and irrevocable as this love (cf. *AAS* 71 [1979], p. 1224). This truth is a great consolation for the world, and because some marriages fail, there is an ever greater need for the Church and all her members to proclaim it faithfully.

Christ Himself, the living source of grace and mercy, is close to all those whose marriage has known trial, pain, or anguish. Throughout the ages countless married people have drawn from the Paschal Mystery of Christ's cross and resurrection the strength to bear Christian witness—at times very difficult—to the indissolubility of Christian marriage. And all the efforts of the Christian people to bear faithful witness to God's law, despite human weakness, have not been in vain. These efforts are the human response made, through grace, to a God who has first loved us and who has given Himself for us.

As I explained in my Apostolic Exhortation *Familiaris consortio*, the Church is vitally concerned for the pastoral care of the family in all difficult cases. We must reach out with love—the love of Christ—to those who know the pain of failure in marriage; to those who know the loneliness of bringing up a family on their own; to those whose family life is dominated by tragedy or by illness of mind or body. I praise all those who help people wounded by the breakdown of their marriage, by showing them Christ's compassion and counseling them according to Christ's truth.

7. To the public authorities, and to all men and women of good will, I say: treasure your families. Protect their rights. Support the family by your laws and administration. Allow the voice of the family to be heard in the making of your policies. The future of your society, the future of humanity, passes by way of the family.

8. My brothers and sisters in Christ, who are now about to renew the promises of your wedding day: may your words express once more the truth that is in your heart and may they generate faithful love within your families. Make sure that your families are real communities of love. Allow that love to reach out to other people, near and far. Reach out especially to the lonely and burdened people of your neighborhood, to the poor and to all those on the margin of society. In this way you will build up your society in peace, for peace requires trust, and trust is the child of love, and love comes to birth in the cradle of the family.

Today and always, may God bless all of you, and all the families of Britain. Amen.

And how can we not recall those many families in Britain and in Argentina who bear the heavy weight of pain and sorrow because of the loss of their loved ones in the South Atlantic. As we ask God to comfort them in their affliction, let us pray for peace, a just and lasting peace, so that other families may be spared the sufferings of war, so that other husbands, wives and children may not have to surrender what is most sacred in the community of the family, love and life. Amen.

Let Your Lives Be Formed by the Holy Spirit

A joyful encounter with young people of Scotland took place on the afternoon of May 31 where thousands had gathered at Murrayfield Stadium, in Edinburgh. The Holy Father spoke to the group as follows:

Dear young people of Scotland!

1. Thank you for such warm words of welcome. I am happy that my first contact is with you, the pride of your beloved country and the promise of its bright future!

You are at the great crossroads of your lives and you must decide how your future can be lived happily, accepting the responsibilities which you hope will be placed squarely on your shoulders, playing an active role in the world around you. You ask me for encouragement and guidance, and most willingly I offer some words of advice to all of you, in the name of Jesus Christ.

In the first place I say this: you must never think that you are alone in deciding your future!

And secondly: when deciding your future, you must not decide for yourself alone!

2. There is an episode in the life of St. Andrew, the patron saint of Scotland, which can serve as an example for what I wish to tell you. Jesus had been teaching a crowd of five thousand people about the kingdom of God. They had listened carefully all day, and as evening approached He did not want to send them away hungry, so He told His disciples to give

them something to eat. He said this really to test them, because He knew exactly what He was going to do. One of the disciples—it was St. Andrew—said: "There is a small boy here with five barley loaves and two fishes; but what is that among so many?" Jesus took the loaves, blessed them, and gave them out to all who were sitting waiting; He then did the same with the fish, giving out as much as was wanted. Later the disciples collected twelve baskets of the fragments that were left over (cf. Jn. 6:1-14).

Now the point I wish to make is this: St. Andrew gave Jesus all there was available, and Jesus miraculously fed those five thousand people and still had something left over. It is exactly the same with your lives. Left alone to face the difficult challenges of life today, you feel conscious of your inadequacy and afraid of what the future may hold for you. But what I say to you is this: place your lives in the hands of Jesus. He will accept you, and bless you, and He will make such use of your lives as will be beyond your greatest expectations! In other words: surrender yourselves, like so many loaves and fishes, into the all-powerful, sustaining hands of God and you will find yourselves transformed with "newness of life" (Rom. 6:4), with fullness of life (cf. Jn. 1:16). "Unload your burden on the Lord, and he will support you" (Ps. 55:22).

LET JESUS FORM YOU

3. It is not of primary importance what walk of life naturally attracts you—industry or commerce, science or engineering, medicine or nursing, the priestly or religious life, or the law, or teaching, or

some other form of public service—the principle remains always the same: hand the direction of your life over to Jesus and allow Him to transform you and obtain the best results, the one He wishes from you.

Only Christianity has given a religious meaning to work and recognizes the spiritual value of technological progress. There is no vocation more religious than work! St. Benedict used to say to his monks that every implement in the monastery must be regarded as a sacred vessel. A Catholic layman or laywoman is someone who takes work seriously. Why? Because, as St. Paul says, "I live now not with my own life, but with the life of Christ who lives in me" (Gal. 2:20); "Life to me is Christ" (Phil. 1:21).

4. How can this be? That is a good question. Our Blessed Lady, Mary of Nazareth, asked that very same question when God's extraordinary plan for her life was first explained to her. And the answer which Mary received from Almighty God is the identical answer that He gives to you: "The Holy Spirit will come upon you and the power of the Most High will cover you with its shadow...nothing is impossible to God" (Lk. 1:34-37).

This is the one same Holy Spirit who came to you at Baptism and again, with increased vigor, at Confirmation, precisely to prepare and fortify you for the challenge of life. Not one of you is without Him! No one must ever feel alone! The Spirit of the Lord has been given to you! (cf. Lk. 4:18)

Who is this Holy Spirit? He is God Himself. The Third Person of the Blessed Trinity. He is sent to each of us by the Father and the Son. He is their greatest gift and He remains constantly with us. He abides in us.

We have difficulty in forming a concept of the Holy Spirit in our mind. It is of the highest importance, however, that we have some understanding of His influence and His activity in our lives.

GIFTS OF THE SPIRIT

5. The clearest description of the work of the Holy Spirit has been given by St. Paul, who said that the Spirit produces "love, joy, peace, patience, kindness, goodness, trustfulness, gentleness and self-control" (Gal. 5:22). *Qualities such as these are ideal in every walk of life and in all circumstances:* at home, with your parents and brothers and sisters; at school, with your teachers and friends; in the factory or at the university; with all the people you meet.

The prophet Isaiah also attributed special gifts to the Holy Spirit: "a spirit of wisdom and understanding, a spirit of counsel and fortitude, a spirit of knowledge and fear of the Lord" (Is. 11:2). St. Paul is right in saying: "Since the Spirit is our life, let us be directed by the Spirit" (Gal. 5:25).

6. With gifts and qualities such as these we are equal to any task and capable of overcoming any difficulties. Yet our lives remain our own, and the Spirit acts on each of us differently, in harmony with our individual personality and the characteristics we have inherited from our parents and from the upbringing received in our homes.

If you pause to reflect for a moment or two you will begin to realize how much you experience the presence of the Holy Spirit in your lives, especially through the goodness and kindness that other people show to you, even though you do not actually see Him in the world. The Holy Spirit is a living Spirit and His action is interwoven with all the realities of our lives, so that daily we encounter Him in other people, but also in particular happenings and in the things of nature, which so frequently direct our thoughts to God. And my visit to you today, our being together, is a work of the Holy Spirit.

TO AID OUR WEAKNESS

7. Because He is so near to us, yet so unobtrusive, we should turn to the Holy Spirit instinctively in all our needs and ask Him for His guidance and help. God has sent Him to us because of our helplessness, as St. Paul says so beautifully: "The Spirit too comes to help us in our weakness. For when we cannot choose words in order to pray properly, the Spirit Himself expresses our plea in a way that could never be put into words" (Rom. 8:26). What more could God do for us? What more can we expect of God than that?

8. If the Holy Spirit were to be withdrawn then we would immediately notice the difference. St. Paul tells us what happens when we refuse to be guided by the Spirit: "When self-indulgence is at work the results are obvious: fornication, gross indecency and sexual irresponsibility...feuds and wrangling, jealousy, bad temper and quarrels; disagreements, factions, envy, drunkenness, orgies and similar things. I warn you now, as I warned you before: those who behave like this will not inherit the kingdom of God" (Gal. 5:19-21).

This too is part of the liberating Good News of the Gospel. A correct understanding of the teaching of

Jesus makes us react in a creative and cooperative fashion to the challenges that face us in life, without fear of acting mistakenly and alone, but under the guiding influence of His own Holy Spirit at every moment and in every circumstance, be it great or small.

EXTRAORDINARY HELP

9. This extraordinary divine assistance is guaranteed to all who offer their lives to Jesus. God the Father's plan of salvation embraces all mankind; His one same Holy Spirit is sent as a gift to all who are open to receive Him in faith. We each form a part of God's over-all plan. An exclusively personal and private attitude to salvation is not Christian and is born of a fundamentally mistaken mentality.

Consequently, your lives cannot be lived in isolation, and even in deciding your future you must always keep in mind your responsibility as Christians towards others. There is no place in your lives for apathy or indifference to the world around you. There is no place in the Church for selfishness. You must show a conscientious concern that the standards of society fit the plan of God. Christ counts on you, so that the effects of His Holy Spirit may radiate from you to others and in that way permeate every aspect of the public and the private sector of national life. "To each is given the manifestation of the Spirit for the common good" (1 Cor. 12:7).

10. Do not let the sight of the world in turmoil shake your confidence in Jesus. Not even the threat of nuclear war. Remember His words: "Be brave: I have conquered the world" (Jn. 16:33). Let no temptation

discourage you. Let no failure hold you down. There is nothing that you cannot master with the help of the One who gives you strength (cf. Phil. 4:13).

11. Follow the example of our Blessed Lady, the perfect model of trust in God and wholehearted cooperation in His divine plan for the salvation of mankind. Keep in mind the advice she gave the servants at Cana: "Do whatever he tells you" (Jn. 2:5). Jesus changed the water into wine for His Mother on that occasion. Through her intercession He will transform your lives.

I must continue now with my pilgrimage through your beloved Scotland. I take leave of you happy in the thought that your young hearts accompany me on my journey, and that I have the support of your daily prayers. For my part I wish to assure you, each and every one of you, of my love in Christ Jesus.

Young people of Scotland, I thank you. Keep the Faith joyfully; and my blessing be with you.

Oigridh na h-Alba, tha mi toirt taing dhùibh.
Cumaibh an creideamh gu sòlasach;
agus mo bheannachd leibh.

Love for Our Sacred Calling

Pope John Paul met the priests and religious of Scotland in Edinburgh Cathedral on the evening of May 31. In response to the greeting of Cardinal Gordon Joseph Gray, Archbishop of Edinburgh, the Pope spoke as follows:

My brothers and sisters in Christ,

1. As the Church celebrates Mary's great song of praise to God, the *Magnificat,* I am very happy to be with you in this cathedral dedicated to her name. I thank God for your love of Christ and your commitment to His Church.

You represent all the priests and men and women religious of Scotland. You are the closest collaborators of the bishops in their pastoral ministry. You are present in every area of the community's life, hastening the coming of the kingdom of God through your prayer and work. In you I feel the heartbeat of the entire ecclesial community. In your lives I read the history of the Church in this land, a history of much faith and love. I recognize the contribution made by priests and religious from other lands, especially from Ireland, who have helped to strengthen the Catholic community here. Your presence speaks of hope and vitality for the future.

During my pastoral visits to the various countries of the world, my meeting with the priests and religious are special moments of ecclesial significance.

And today, once again, I am able to fulfill my task: to confirm you in the faith (cf. Lk. 22:31), and to remind you, with St. Peter, that you have been born anew to a living hope, to an inheritance that is imperishable (cf. 1 Pt. 1:4).

2. My greeting goes in the first place to the priests, both diocesan and religious, sharers in the one priesthood of Christ the High Priest, "appointed to act on behalf of men in relation to God, to offer gifts and sacrifices for sins" (Heb. 5:1). Your presence gives me great joy and fraternal support. In you I recognize the good shepherd, the faithful servant, the sower who goes out to sow the good seed, the laborer in the vineyard, the fisherman who launches his net for a catch. You are Christ's close friends: "I call you friends, not servants, for the servant does not know his Master's business" (Jn. 15:15).

As priests we must recognize the mystery of grace in our lives. As St. Paul puts it, we have this ministry "by the mercy of God" (2 Cor. 4:1). It is a gift. It is an act of trust on Christ's part, calling us to be "stewards of the mysteries of God" (1 Cor. 4:1). It is a sacramental configuration with Christ the High Priest. The priesthood is not ours to do with as we please. We cannot reinvent its meaning according to our personal views. Ours is to be true to the One who has called us.

The priesthood is a gift to us. But in us and through us the priesthood is a gift to the Church. Let us never separate our priestly life and ministry from full and wholehearted communion with the whole Church. Brothers in the priestly ministry, what does the Church expect from you? The Church expects that you and your brothers and sisters, the religious, will be the first to love her, to hear her voice and follow her inspiration, so that the people of our time may be served effectively.

3. As priests you are at the service of Christ the Teacher (cf. PO 1). A very important part of your ministry is to preach and teach the Christian message. In the passage that I have already mentioned, St. Paul describes his own attitude to this ministry: "We refuse to tamper with God's word, but by the open statement of the truth we would commend ourselves to every man's conscience in the sight of God" (2 Cor. 4:2). *We must not tamper with God's Word.* We must strive to apply the Good News to the ever-changing conditions of the world but, courageously and at all costs, we must resist the temptation to alter its content, or reinterpret it in order to make it fit the spirit of the present age. The message we preach is not the wisdom of this world (cf. 1 Cor. 1:20), but the words of life that seem like foolishness to the unspiritual man (cf. *ibid.,* 2:14). "In their case," Paul continues, "the god of this world has blinded the minds of the unbelievers, to keep them from seeing the light of the Gospel of the glory of Christ, who is the likeness of God" (2 Cor. 4:4). He goes on: "For what we preach is not ourselves, but Jesus Christ as Lord" (v. 5).

We should not be surprised then if our message of conversion and life is not always well-received. Do everything in your power to present the Word as effectively as possible, believe in the power of the Word itself, and never become discouraged: "The kingdom of God is as if a man should scatter seed upon the ground and should sleep and rise night and day, and the seed should sprout and grow he knows not how" (Mk. 4:26-27). Yet, in another sense, we do know how the seed grows: "God gives the growth" (1 Cor. 3:7). In this sense we are "God's fellow workers" (v. 6). How careful we must be about our preaching! It should be the continuation of our prayer.

4. We priests share in the priesthood of Christ. We are His ministers, His instruments. But it is Christ who in the sacraments, especially in the Eucharist, offers divine life to mankind (cf. PO 5). With what care, with what love must we celebrate the sacred mysteries! The sacredness of what takes place in our liturgical celebrations must not be obscured. These celebrations must be an experience of prayer and ecclesial communion for all who take part in them.

I know of the many efforts being made to ensure ecclesial renewal according to the directives of the Second Vatican Council. I encourage you to continue to develop among the laity a sense of shared responsibility for the liturgical and apostolic life of your parishes. Through their spiritual priesthood, the laity are called to take their proper place in the Church's life according to the grace and charism given to each one. Lead them in the Faith. Inspire them and encourage them to work for the well-being and growth of the ecclesial family; their contribution is extremely important. Encourage the young, especially, to "desire the higher gifts" (1 Cor. 12:31). Work closely with them, and also show them the challenge and attractiveness of the priesthood and the religious life.

5. To spend your lives in the service of the People of God, through word and sacrament: this is your great task, your glory, your treasure. But it is St. Paul

again who reminds us: "We have this treasure in earthen vessels" (2 Cor. 4:7). The personal experience of each of us is that our joy and fruitfulness in the priestly life come from a full acceptance of our priestly identity. We must love our vocation and mission, but we must also *be seen* to love our priesthood. Let your people see that you are men of prayer. Let them see that you treat the sacred mysteries with love and respect. Let them see that your commitment to peace, justice and truth is sincere, unconditional and brave. Let everyone see that you love the Church, and that you are of one mind and heart with her. What is at stake is the credibility of our witness!

6. Brothers and sisters, members of the religious communities! How I wish I could greet each of you personally! To hear from each one of you the *"magnalia Dei,"* how the Holy Spirit works in your lives! In the depths of your hearts, in the struggle between grace and sin, in the various moments and circumstances of your pilgrimage of faith—in how many ways has Christ spoken to you and said: "Come, follow me"! Could the Pope come to Scotland and not say thank you for having answered that call? Of course not! So, thank you on behalf of the Church. Thank you for the specific witness you give and for all the gifts you contribute.

Because you have carried your baptismal grace to a degree of "total dedication to God by an act of supreme love" in religious consecration (cf. LG 44), you have become a sign of a higher life, a "life that is more than food, a body that is more than clothing" (Lk. 12:23). Through the practice of the evangelical counsels you have become a prophetic sign of the eternal kingdom of the Father. In the midst of the world you point to the "one thing that is needed" (Lk. 10:42), to the "treasure that does not fail" (Lk. 12:33). You possess the source of inspiration and of strength for the various forms of apostolic work which your institutes are called to carry out.

7. Those of you who belong to contemplative communities serve the People of God "in the heart of Christ." You prophetically remind those engaged in building up the earthly city that, unless they lay its foundation in the Lord, they will have labored in vain (cf. LG 46). Yours is a striking witness to the Gospel message, all the more necessary since the people of our time often succumb to a false sense of independence with respect to the Creator. Your lives testify to the absolute primacy of God and to the kingship of Christ.

8. And you, brothers and sisters, whose vocation is active work in ecclesial service, you must combine contemplation with apostolic zeal. By contemplative prayer you cling to God in mind and heart; by apostolic love and zeal you associate yourselves with the work of redemption and you spread the kingdom of God (cf. PC 5). In your service to the human family you must take care not to confuse the *Regnum Dei* with the *Regnum hominis,* as if political, social and economic liberation were the same as salvation in Jesus Christ (cf. John Paul I, General Audience, September 20, 1978). Your prophetic role in the Church should lead you to discover and proclaim the deepest meaning of all human activity. Only when human activity preserves its relationship with the Creator does it preserve its dignity and reach fulfillment.

Your communities have been engaged in the process of renewal desired by the Second Vatican Council. You are trying to be ever more faithful to your role within the ecclesial community, in accordance with your specific charisms. Proceeding from the original inspiration of your founders and following the Magisterium of the Church, you are in an excellent position to discern the promptings of the Holy Spirit regarding the needs of the Church and the world today. Through appropriate exterior adaptation accompanied by constant spiritual conversion, your life and activity, within the context of the local and universal Church, become magnificent expressions of the Church's own vitality and youth.

In the word's of St. Paul: "I thank my God through Jesus Christ for all of you, because your faith is proclaimed in all the world" (Rom. 1:8).

9. Brothers and sisters, there is one who walks beside us along the path of discipleship: Mary, the Mother of Jesus, who pondered everything in her heart and always did the will of the Father (cf. Lk. 2:51; Mk. 3:35). In this Metropolitan Cathedral dedicated to her, I wish to return to the thoughts and sentiments that filled my heart at Fatima on May 13. There I once again consecrated to her myself and my ministry: *Totus Tuus Ego Sum.* I reconsecrated, and entrusted to her maternal protection, the Church and the whole world, so much in need of wisdom and peace.

These are some of the invocations I addressed to the Immaculate Heart of Mary at Fatima:

"From famine and war, *deliver us.*

"From nuclear war, from incalculable self-destruction, from every kind of war, *deliver us.*

"From sins against the life of man from its very beginning, *deliver us.*

"From hatred and from the demeaning of the dignity of the children of God, *deliver us.*

"From every kind of injustice in the life of society, both national and international, *deliver us.*

"From readiness to trample on the commandments of God, *deliver us.*

"From attempts to stifle in human hearts the very truth of God, *deliver us.*

"From sins against the Holy Spirit, *deliver us, deliver us.*

"Accept, O Mother of Christ, this cry laden with the sufferings of all individual human beings, laden with the sufferings of whole societies.

"Let there be revealed, once more, in the history of the world the infinite power of merciful love. May it put a stop to evil. May it transform consciences. May your Immaculate Heart reveal for all the light of hope."

And to each priest and deacon, to each religious brother and sister, to each seminarian, I leave a word of encouragement and a message of hope. With Saint Paul I say to you: "This explains why we work and struggle as we do; our hopes are fixed on the living God..." (1 Tm. 4:10). Yes, dear brothers and sisters, our hopes are fixed on the living God!

May Our Desire for Unity Be Hope for a Divided World

In the early morning of June 1, the Holy Father received at the archbishop's residence in Edinburgh representatives of other Christian Churches in Scotland. He addressed them as follows:

"The grace of our Lord Jesus Christ be with your spirit, brethren" (Gal. 6:18).

1. It is a joy to meet with you this morning and I am very appreciative of your courtesy in coming at this early hour. Yesterday, soon after my arrival in Scotland, I had the happiness of being greeted by the Moderator of the General Assembly of the Church of Scotland, the Right Reverend Professor John McIntyre. In this regard, I cannot fail to recall that first historic meeting in 1961 between the then Moderator, Doctor Archibald Craig, and my own Predecessor, John XXIII; or the courtesy of Dr. Peter Brodie during his moderatorial year in attending, in 1978, both my own installation and that of John Paul I. I am aware too of the significance of last night's happy venue, the precincts of the assembly hall itself, the seat of the Church of Scotland's Supreme Court, and also the *locus* of that momentous meeting in 1910 of the World Missionary Conference which is generally regarded as marking the beginning of the modern ecumenical movement.

2. It was in that same spirit of prayerful ecumenical endeavor that I also had the great pleasure last Saturday of meeting representatives of the Church of Scotland and the Episcopal Church in Scotland, together with other British church leaders. I am sure that you will agree with me that such meetings as this have an importance of their own; the very fact that they take place is a witness before the world that, despite the sad history of division between Christ's followers, all of us who worship the one true God are desirous today of collaborating in the name of God and of working together for the promotion of the human values of which He is the true Author.

3. In particular I have been pleased to learn of the fruitful dialogues in which the Catholic Church in this country has been engaged with the Church of Scotland, the Episcopal Church in Scotland and other Churches, and also of its collaboration with the Scottish Churches' Council in many aspects of its work. I would like to make special mention of the Joint Commissions on Doctrine and on Marriage with the Church of Scotland and the Joint Study Group with the Scottish Episcopal Church, members of which groups are present here this morning. May I express my appreciation for your patient and painstaking work in the name of Christ. Here too we have an instance of that common witness which is both an expression of the degree of unity, limited but real, which we already enjoy through God's grace, and of our sincere desire to follow the ways by which God is leading us to that full unity which He alone can give. In following this road we have still to overcome many obstacles occasioned by the sad history of past enmities; we have to resolve important doctrinal issues;

OUR DESIRE FOR UNITY 131

yet already mutual love, our will for unity, can be a sign of hope to a divided world—not least in these days in which peace is so sorely imperiled.

I have looked forward to this meeting. Brief though it is, it offers us an opportunity to greet one another as brethren and, most important of all, to join in prayer that He who has begun this good work in us will bring it to completion (cf. Phil. 1:6).

I am happy to greet also the representative of the Jewish community in Scotland who, by his presence here, symbolizes the deep spiritual links which bind our two religious communities so closely together (cf. NA 4).

I welcome in the same way the representative of the Islamic communities in this country, and I am happy to recall the religious values we have in common, as believers in the one almighty and merciful God (cf. NA 3). May He show His face to us and give us peace!

Assisting the Handicapped —a Sign of Communion

Before leaving Edinburgh for Glasgow, the Holy Father made a brief visit to St. Joseph's Hospital of Rosewell where he spoke to the handicapped children and their assistants as follows:

My dear friends and children in Jesus Christ,

1. I am delighted to be making this visit to Saint Joseph's Hospital, Rosewell, and I have come for several reasons. First, to greet you the patients in the care of the hospital, suffering from both mental and physical handicap, and also the Sisters of Charity of St. Vincent de Paul who administer the hospital, with the medical advisers, nursing and auxiliary staff, chaplains and volunteer workers for the handicapped in general, and the parents and families of those who are receiving this special care.

Another reason for my visit is to bear witness to the Church's mission from Christ to care for all God's people, especially those most in need. I am interested to know that the ancient Gaelic language of Scotland has a most telling phrase, *corramaich fo chùram Dhè*, which speaks of the handicapped as living under God's protection—"God's handicapped." Such a sensitive description, or title, captures a whole variety of profoundly Christian insights into the meaning of life and its dignity, a life which all of us have received from the Creator and whose course we share in various ways as separate individuals. And what is more, for the baptized this is a new life of grace in and through Jesus Christ, the Savior of the world.

2. Those who do not enjoy the fullness of what is called a normal way of life, through either mental or serious physical handicap, are often compensated in part by qualities which people often take for granted or even distort, under the influence of a materialistic society: such things as a radiant love—transparent, innocent and yearning—and the attraction of loving and selfless care. In this regard, we often find in the Gospels the refreshing example of Jesus Himself, and the loving bond of affection between Him and the sick or disabled: how many were His exertions for them, the great words of faith addressed to them, and His wonderful interventions on their behalf, "for power came forth from him" (Lk. 6:19; cf. Mk. 1:32-34). There were times when He went out of His way to identify Himself with the sick and the suffering, He who was to suffer such a passion and death Himself: "I was sick and you visited me.... As you did it to one of the least of these my brethren, you did it to me" (Mt. 25:36, 40).

3. These latter words of Jesus are also a source of great consolation to all those who care for the sick and disabled: nurses and medical staff, sisters and chaplains, parents, volunteer helpers and friends. For your loving care and self-sacrifice are all too often a source of your own suffering, through tiredness, emotional and mental strain, and other such burdens. So much so that, when you identify with the handicapped in your loving and attentive service to them, you also share the accolade of St. Paul: "In my flesh I make up what is lacking in Christ's afflictions for the sake

of his body, that is, the church" (Col. 1:24; cf. 2 Cor. 1:5; 12:19). And when you really feel at your lowest ebb, our Lord Himself has a further and very personal message of comfort: "Come to me, all who labor and are heavy-laden, and I will give you rest. Take my yoke upon you, and learn from me; for I am gentle and lowly in heart, and you will find rest for your souls. For my yoke is easy, and my burden is light" (Mt. 11:28-30). These words of encouragement from Christ, which I pass on to you in His name, are meant also for those who are caring for the handicapped at home, and trying to give them as normal a family life as possible.

4. I know from Cardinal Gray that this Archdiocese of St. Andrew's and Edinburgh, as well as other dioceses in Scotland, provides a reassuring and supportive role through special Masses and reunions for the handicapped and their helpers at regular intervals in various parish centers. In this spirit of Christian cooperation and service, you are admirably obeying the call to rejoice with those who rejoice and to suffer with those who suffer (cf. Rom. 12:15). This offers not only a stimulus to a truly human and humanizing disposition, but also a sign of communion that enriches both the one who gives and the one who receives.

5. No visit to Rosewell would be complete without mentioning a young woman whose holy life and final suffering gave full expression to the message from Sacred Scripture that we have reflected on this morning: the Venerable Margaret Sinclair, known later in the religious life as Sister Mary Francis of the Five Wounds, Poor Clare Colletine, who lived from 1900

until 1925. For it was to Rosewell that Margaret came on holidays with other members of her family from their home in Edinburgh. Margaret could well be described as one of God's little ones who, through her very simplicity, was touched by God with the strength of real holiness of life, whether as a child, a young woman, an apprentice, a factory worker, member of a trade union, or a professed sister in religion. How appropriate it is then that Rosewell should be chosen for the location of the Margaret Sinclair Center, the purpose of which is to make her inspiring example better known and to promote her cause for beatification. I fully appreciate the aspirations of the Catholics of Scotland, and elsewhere, for that singular event to be realized, and I know that you are praying that it may come about.

With this recollection of the Venerable Margaret Sinclair, I leave you with her inspiration. In drawing us to love and assist the handicapped, the Lord Jesus touches our lives with His strength, and finally rewards us according to His promise: "As you did it to one of the least of these my brethren, you did it to me" (Mt. 25:40).

Praised be Jesus Christ!

The Cause of Catholic Education

In St. Andrew's College, Glasgow, on June 1, Pope John Paul met a large group of teachers and students from various Catholic institutes and addressed them as follows:

My brothers and sisters in Jesus Christ,

1. It is a great joy to me to have this opportunity to greet you here on this beautiful campus of Saint Andrew's College of Education, at Bearsden, Glasgow. I wish also to express my cordial esteem to the distinguished representatives of the civil and educational authorities of Scotland here present with the staff and students of the college, their parents, clergy and religious, and associates from the schools, universities, colleges of further education, and other institutions of educational science.

St. Andrew's College, as I understand, has quite recently been formed from two splendid traditions of teacher-training: Notre Dame College of Education here at Bearsden and Dowanhill, Glasgow, and Craiglockhart College of Education in Edinburgh. As a national college now, it enjoys the same patron as Scotland itself, the Apostle St. Andrew, the brother of Simon Peter, with whom the momentous invitation was received from the Lord almost two thousand years ago: "Come, follow me and I will make you fishers of men" (Mk. 1:17).

Today, the Successor of St. Peter finds himself in the gracious company of the spiritual sons and daughters of Andrew, here in your beautiful Scotland. And although I too am a "man from a far country," I am not unaware of the rich heritage of Scotland and of this great city of Glasgow and the surrounding region of Strathclyde. Glasgow, the city of St. Kentigern or Mungo (the good man), whom history regards as its first bishop, dates from as early as the sixth century. A city whose famous medieval University has emblazoned on its arms the words of Christ Himself—*"Via, Veritas, Vita"*—of Him who is truly "the way, the truth and the life" (Jn. 14:16).

PAST ACHIEVEMENTS

This most pleasant venue causes us to reflect on the importance long given in Scotland to the promotion of sound education, and to consider the implications of this for the present and immediate future.

2. To mention only a few of the achievements of the past, one thinks of the contribution of Saint Margaret in the eleventh century, that gifted queen and patroness of Scotland; the founding of the Universities of St. Andrew's, Glasgow and Aberdeen (King's College) in the fifteenth century; the choir of *"sang schull"* and the grammar schools of the same period; and the subsequent parish schools throughout the land, where the *"Dominie"* or master gave every encouragement to the *"lad o' pairts."* Not only did Scotland's sons and daughters eventually bring education to the distant countries of the Commonwealth, but so also have not a few leaders of developing countries been trained in your ancient universities, including Edinburgh, and your more recent foundations like Strathclyde, Stirling and Heriot-Watt. One notes in

particular the long-standing concern of the established Church of Scotland for suitable educational provision at all levels, and we rejoice in its committees' increasing collaboration with the Catholic Church, not least in the field of religious education.

Worthy of special mention, I feel, are the statutory provisions of the education (Scotland) Act of 1918, whereby Catholic schools are a constituent part of the state system, with essential guarantees covering religious education and the appointment of teachers. In this context, I wish to pay tribute to the religious and lay teachers whose dedication paved the way for this system, not forgetting the vision of the civil and ecclesiastical authorities who brought it about, as also their patient discretion in implementing it.

While Catholic teachers and their confreres can take just pride in past achievements, I am sure their realism is no less than that of Thomas Reid and the Scottish "Common Sense" school of philosophy; for common sense alone would exclude any temptation to complacency, not least in view of rapid developments in the social and economic order.

Obviously any sound educational philosophy would have to take all this into account.

PERSPECTIVE MISSING

3. It would seem to be the case that in modern times the success of a particular educational program or system has been measured, to a large extent, by the recognized qualification it provided with a view to some career prospect. This would appear to be felt most in the secondary sector of education, where

direction for future prospects is crucial. Hence the emphasis, until now, on a certificate-oriented curriculum, with the certificate seen as the virtual guarantee of career expectations.

Such an outlook has tended to encourage an "outward" trend in education—not itself a bad thing, but a certain balance or perspective has been missing: the perspective of the whole person, his inner self as well as his outer prospects.

But nowadays, as we have been made only too aware, the possession of a certificate does not bring automatic employment. Indeed, this harsh reality has brought about not only deep frustration among young people, many of whom have worked so hard, but also a sense of malaise in the educational system itself. Hence the question: what has gone wrong? What has specialization achieved in our day—in real terms, in terms of life? Wherein lies the remedy?

FITTED FOR LIFE

4. Perhaps we could reflect on the philosophy behind education: education as the completing of the person. To be educated is to be more fitted for life; to have a greater capacity for appreciating what life is, what it has to offer, and what the person has to offer in return to the wider society of man. Thus, if we would apply our modern educational skills and resources to this philosophy, we might succeed in offering something of lasting value to our pupils and students, an antidote to often immediate prospects of frustration and boredom, not to mention the uncertainty of the long-term future.

I am given to understand that educationalists and educational authorities in Scotland have already come to terms with this problem and are giving due emphasis to education as development of the whole person; not only intellectual ability, but also emotional, physical and social development. These integral aspects are, I believe, an ever recurring theme in various official reports. So what I have to say this morning is by way of moral support and encouragement for the continuing work of implementing these recommendations at every level in the school sector, both primary and secondary. I appreciate too that this task of educational development is itself hindered by serious economic factors that impinge very much on staffing provision and material resources. But one cannot but recognize, and welcome, the encouraging factors evidenced by the educational developments themselves.

First and foremost must surely be the increasing involvement of parents, especially in the primary and secondary sectors, and also, if to a lesser extent, in the tertiary sector. In some ways, this has been realized through the structures of Parent/Teacher Associations or similar bodies: the concept of community schools; the opening of school libraries and leisure facilities to parents; and through this, the wonderful opportunity for adult or continuing education—towards the full development of the person and his or her God-given potential.

It is only right that parents should be more involved in educational structures. For are not parents, in the sight of God, the primary educators of their children? Such a basic principle was underscored by the Second Vatican Council, in particular in the Declaration on Christian Education: "Since it is the parents who have given life to their children, it is they who have the serious obligation of educating their offspring. Hence parents must be recognized as the first and foremost educators of their children" (GE 3).

The promotion of this "integrated, personal and social" education is also, we need hardly mention, the necessary and complementary role of the school. And here, in the day-to-day progress towards objectives, are to be found real elements of encouragement too.

In realizing that consideration for the "whole person" involves his spiritual dimension, one notes that the Scottish education authorities, apart from already approving courses and qualifications for specialist teachers in religious education, are giving serious attention to other provisions like national examinations and the services of Her Majesty's Inspectorate. And it is especially heartening to learn that the Education Committee of the General Assembly of the Church of Scotland and the Roman Catholic Education Commission have undertaken a united approach regarding important aspects of this deliberation.

"THE CATHOLIC SCHOOL"

5. The issues focused on above, especially the development of the whole person, the spiritual dimension of education, and the involvement of parents, have always been central to the ethos of the Catholic school. This has been particularly true of the primary school, with the close bond between the family, school, parish and local community. Nor has this been absent in the more complex situation of the

secondary sector, where the diocese often provides chaplains, above all for the school as a community of faith centered on the Eucharist and also, where possible, to serve as a pastoral link with the local parishes. However, always mindful of the constant need for improvement, the Catholic school ought to make full use of suitable new opportunities available, for no other reason than to fulfill its own identity and role. And we do well at this point to recollect what precisely is the identity and purpose of the Catholic school.

Such a reminder is conveniently provided in the document of that title, *The Catholic School*, published by the Holy See's Sacred Congregation for Christian Education in March 1977: The Catholic school, it declares, "is committed...to the development of the whole man, since in Christ, the Perfect Man, all human values find their fulfillment and unity. Herein lies the specifically Catholic character of the school. Its duty to cultivate human values in their own legitimate right in accordance with its particular mission to serve all men has its origin in the figure of Christ.... Its task is fundamentally a synthesis of culture and faith, and a synthesis of faith and life" *(op. cit.*, 35-37).

Implicit throughout these terms of reference for the Catholic school is the imperative of Christian commitment on the part of its teachers. The Catholic school "must be a community whose aim is the transmission of values for living. Its work is seen as promoting a faith relationship with Christ in whom all values find fulfillment. But faith is principally assimilated through contact with people whose daily life bears witness to it" *(op. cit.*, 53).

In reflecting on the value of Catholic schools and the importance of Catholic teachers and educators, it is necessary to stress the central point of Catholic education itself. Catholic education is above all a question of communicating Christ, of helping to form Christ in the lives of others. Those who have been baptized must be trained to live the newness of Christian life in justice and in the holiness of truth. The cause of Catholic education is the cause of Jesus Christ and of His Gospel at the service of man.

Nor must we ignore the integrity of the catechetical message as taught: "The person who becomes a disciple of Christ has the right to receive the word of faith' (Rom. 10:8) not in mutilated, falsified or diminished form but whole and entire.... Thus no true catechist can lawfully, on his own initiative, make a selection of what he considers important in the deposit of faith as opposed to what he considers unimportant, so as to teach the one and reject the other.... The method and language used must truly be means for communicating the whole and not just part of 'the words of eternal life' (Jn. 6:68; cf. Acts 5:20; 7:38) and the 'ways of life' (Acts 2:28, quoting Ps. 16:11)..." (CT 30-31).

THE WHOLE TRUTH

6. Whereas most of my address has centered on the crucial area of the school, with obvious implications for teacher-training, I would hope that those here present from the universities would recognize, with this former university professor, the relevance of the school for the university: not merely as a

recruiting-ground for students, but as an essential part of the continuing process of education.

As for the university itself, I would simply like to mention some points I have had occasion to make on this topic, to the general conference of UNESCO, to various university groups in Rome, and in Bologna only last April. I feel that the last mentioned is particularly appropriate, since I am told that it was the University of Bologna which provided the ancient Scottish universities with significant elements of their splendid tradition.

From its very origins and by reason of its institution, the purpose of the university is the acquiring of a scientific knowledge of the truth, of the whole truth. Thus it constitutes one of the fundamental means which man has devised to meet his need for knowledge. But, as the Second Vatican Council observed, "Today it is more difficult than it once was to synthesize the various disciplines of knowledge and the arts. While, indeed, the volume and the diversity of the elements which make up culture increase, at the same time the capacity of individual men to perceive them and to blend them organically decreases, so that the image of universal man becomes even more faint" (GS 61). Any interpretation of knowledge and culture, therefore, which ignores or even belittles the spiritual element of man, his aspirations to the fullness of being, his thirst for truth and the absolute, the questions that he asks himself before the enigmas of sorrow and death, cannot be said to satisfy his deepest and most authentic needs. And since it is in the university that young people experience the high point of their formation education, they should be able to find answers not only about the legitimacy and finality of science but also about higher moral and spiritual values—answers that will restore their confidence in the potential of knowledge gained and the exercise of reason, for their own good and for that of society.

7. By way of summing up, I would like to repeat what I wrote last November in the Apostolic Exhortation on the Family in the Modern World: "It becomes necessary, therefore, on the part of all, to recover an awareness of the primacy of moral values, which are the values of the human person as such. The great task that has to be faced today for the renewal of society is that of recapturing the ultimate meaning of life and its fundamental values" (FC 8).

And as Christians we believe that the ultimate meaning of life and its fundamental values are indeed revealed in Jesus Christ. It is He—Jesus Christ, true God and true man—who says to us: "You call me Teacher and Lord; and you are right, for so I am" (Jn. 13:13-14).

Be Faithful!

Pope John Paul concluded his stay in Glasgow at a concelebrated Mass for the Catholics of Scotland, in Bellahouston Park. The following is the text of the Holy Father's homily during the Mass.

Dear sons and daughters of the Catholic Church in Scotland!

1. Sacred Scripture bears eloquent witness to the unshakable faith which one generation of mankind to the next placed in God. From the time of Abraham onwards through the centuries, that truth remained firmly founded on God's promise to send a Savior who would deliver His people.

Of all the expressions of faith none was more spontaneous than that uttered by Andrew, the fisherman of Galilee: "We have found the Messiah!" (Jn. 1:41) So profound was the impression Jesus made upon him at their first encounter that "early next morning Andrew met his brother and said to him, 'We have found the Messiah'—which means the Christ—and he took Simon to Jesus. Jesus looked hard at him and said, 'You are Simon son of John; you are to be called Cephas—meaning Rock'" (Jn. 1:41-42). It was Andrew, the heavenly patron of your beloved Scotland, who introduced Peter to Jesus!

2. Today marks another significant moment in the history of our salvation: the Successor of Peter comes to visit the spiritual children of Andrew! We are bound one to another by a supernatural brotherhood stronger than that of blood. Here and now we

testify that we profess that identical faith in Jesus, and we firmly hope that we too can lead others to Him. This common profession of faith is the compelling motive behind my pastoral visit to your homeland.

TO ENTER THE KINGDOM

3. Dear brothers and sisters, let us reflect for a few moments on the texts of Sacred Scripture that have been proclaimed in this Liturgy of the Word.

We are gathered here on this Scottish hillside to celebrate Mass. Are we not like those first disciples and followers who sat at the feet of Jesus on the hillside near Capernaum? What did Jesus teach them? What does our Divine Master wish to teach us, each and every one of us, today? With words simple and clear, Jesus outlined the requirements for admission to His heavenly kingdom. He offered reflections on every aspect of daily life. Jesus proposed a new concept of living. In the short introductory phrases to His Sermon on the Mount, Jesus sounded the keynote of the new era He had come to proclaim.

The new spirit is to be gentle, generous, simple, and above all sincere. To avoid being arrogant, censorious, or self-seeking. The disciples of the new kingdom must seek happiness even amidst poverty, deprivation, tears and oppression. To aim for the kingdom requires a radical change in outlook, in mentality, in behavior, in relations with others. Just as the law was revealed to Moses on Mount Sinai, so, in this Sermon on the Mount, Jesus, the new Lawgiver, offers to all mankind a new way of life, a charter of Christian life.

How astonished those first listeners must have been at hearing these dramatic words of Christ! Especially those who were poor in spirit, gentle, or afflicted, downtrodden and oppressed—to hear themselves proclaimed as eligible for entry into a heavenly kingdom.

4. It is this loving fatherhood of God which pervades every word of Jesus. Throughout this discourse He appeals to His listeners to respond to the Father with a response of filial love. Everyone who will be animated by this new spirit is a child of God. This is not the spirit of slaves bringing fear into our lives again; it is the spirit of sons, and it makes us cry out, "Abba, Father" (Rom. 8:14-15). Love can ask more than fear can demand. Love will be the mainspring of the new era. Jesus affirmed this on a later occasion: "If anyone loves me he will keep my word, and my Father will love him, and we shall come to him and make our home with him" (Jn. 14:23).

5. In the qualities required of the true disciples of Jesus we can see the image of Jesus Himself, traced by the prophets in the Old Testament, but described anew in these beatitudes. Quite clearly it was the intention of Jesus that the lives of His disciples should be modeled on His own. "Come to me, all you who labor and are overburdened, and I will give you rest. Shoulder my yoke and learn from me, for I am gentle and humble in heart" (Mt. 11:28-29). While elsewhere He says: "No one can come to the Father except through me" (Jn. 14:6).

EACH IS HAND-PICKED

6. It is essential for us to understand that Jesus has a specific task in life for each and every one of us.

Each one of us is hand-picked, called by name—by Jesus! There is no one among us who does not have a divine vocation! Now this is what St. Paul wrote in his letter to the Ephesians, which was proclaimed a few moments ago: "Each one of us has been given our own share of grace, given as Christ allotted it. And to some, His gift was that they should be apostles; to some, prophets; to some, evangelists; to some, pastors and teachers; so that the saints make a unity in the work of service" (Eph. 4:7, 11-12).

First and foremost, God has called us into existence. He has called us to be! He has called us, through His Son Jesus Christ, to a knowledge of Himself as our loving Father. He has called us to be His children! He has called us to fulfill His eternal plan in our individual lives, with Jesus as our guide. He has called us to be co-heirs with Jesus of His heavenly kingdom! What God our Father is offering us through His Son is a new life as His real children, with Jesus for our Brother; a pressing call to live, to love, to labor for the coming of His kingdom. And lest, bewildered at what we must do, we hesitate, Jesus offers to be Himself our guide and says: "Come, follow me!" (Lk. 9:59)

SCOTLAND'S RESPONSE

7. Dearly beloved in Christ! What response has Scotland given in the past to God's invitation? Christian history narrates that from very early times, perhaps even as early as the second half of the fourth century, Scotland embraced the Gospel of Jesus Christ. For over one thousand five hundred years His holy name has been invoked in this land. St. Ninian,

St. Columba and St. Kentigern were the first to evangelize the pagans and establish a primitive Christian Church. After the Dark Ages had passed, during which the Viking invasions failed to quench the light of the Faith, the coming of Queen Margaret inaugurated a new chapter in the history of the Church in Scotland, which received fresh vigor from internal reorganization and from closer contact with the universal Church.

Although situated geographically on the remote edge of Europe, the Church in Scotland became especially dear to the Popes, at the center and heart of Christianity, and they conferred upon it the exceptional title *Specialis Filia Romanae Ecclesiae,* Special Daughter of the Roman Church! What a magnificent designation!

The Church was intimately involved in the struggle for national independence, with the bishops—men like Robert Wishart of Glasgow—to the forefront of your patriots. And throughout the later Middle Ages our holy Faith continued to flourish in these parts, fine cathedrals and collegiate churches being built, numerous monastic houses being endowed, across the length and breadth of this land. The names of Bishops Wardlaw, Turnbull and Elphinstone remain inseparably linked with the foundation of your universities, of which this little nation has always been so justifiably proud. While Scottish scholars, such as Duns Scotus, Richard of St. Victor and John Major, gained an international repute for learning and brought honor to their native land.

The sixteenth century found the churchmen and the laity unprepared for the religious upheaval of that day, which vehemently swept away the medieval Church from Scotland, almost, though not quite, without trace. The hierarchy became extinct; the remnant of the faithful was dispersed; Scotland was isolated from the reforms decreed by the Council of Trent.

Even this, however, forms part of God's Providence: for the centuries that followed witnessed a valiant struggle for survival, in the face of persecution and exile. To remedy the scarcity of priests, Pope Clement VIII founded a college in Rome for your young countrymen, and similar seminaries were opened in other safe places on the continent, to send laborers back to the "Scottish Mission." The religious orders too released trained members to collaborate in that work. Who has not heard of St. John Ogilvie, the Jesuit, who—only a few miles from where I now stand—surrendered life itself to witness to the Faith of Christ?

The Vicars Apostolic, to whom the organization of all the missionary activity was entrusted, testified in their letters to Rome to the attachment of that handful of Scottish Catholics to the Faith of their fathers, to the See of Peter and to the person of the Pope. Carefully preserved throughout all these years, these documents now serve as a mirror, in which is accurately reflected the noble face of the Scottish Catholic community, lined with the unmistakable signs of poverty and hardship, but radiant with expectation that in God's own time a new day would surely dawn for the Church in Scotland.

Dear beloved Catholics of Scotland, the prayers of your forefathers did not go unanswered! Their firm hope in divine Providence was not disillusioned! A century and a half ago the tide of repression turned. The small Catholic community gradually gained new vitality. The advent of numerous Catholic emigrants from nearby Ireland, accompanied by zealous Irish priests, enlarged and enriched it spiritually. This induced Pope Leo XIII to restore the Catholic hierarchy to Scotland—the very first act of his pontificate—and since that moment there has been a rapid and continuous progress.

HEIRS TO A SACRED HERITAGE

8. You are the heirs to a sacred heritage. Your forefathers have handed on to you the only inheritance they really prized, our holy Catholic Faith! From heaven their heartfelt appeal to you would be this: "Set your hearts on his Kingdom" (Lk. 12:31). With grateful hearts turn to God and thank Him that tranquil days have been restored to the Catholic community in Scotland.

9. What was a dream a century ago has become the reality of today. A complete transformation of Catholic life has come about in Scotland, with the Catholics of Scotland assuming their legitimate role in every sector of public life and some of them invested with the most important and prestigious offices of this land. Is this not what St. Paul has to say to us in today's reading from Ephesians: "So the body grows, until it has built itself up, in love" (Eph 4:16).

You originate in a glorious past, but you do not live in the past. You belong to the present and your generation must not be content simply to rest on the laurels won by your grandparents and great-grandparents. You must give your response to Christ's call to follow Him and enter with Him as co-heirs into His Father's heavenly kingdom. But we find it harder to follow Christ today than appears to have been the case before. Witnessing to Him in modern life means a daily contest, not so quickly and decisively resolved as for the martyrs in the past. As believers we are constantly exposed to pressures by modern society which would compel us to conform to the standards of this secular age, substitute new priorities, restrict our aspirations at the risk of compromising our Christian conscience.

10. The spirit of this world would have us capitulate on the most fundamental principles of our Christian life. Today as never before, the basic doctrines of the Faith are questioned and the value of Christian morality challenged and ridiculed. Things abhorred a generation ago are now inscribed in the statute books of society! These are issues of the utmost gravity to which a simple answer cannot be given; neither are they answered by being ignored. Matters of such magnitude demand the fullest attention of our Christian conscience.

11. To provide the answers to such questions is a daunting task. It would be an impossible challenge for the majority of the faithful to attempt unaided. But you are not alone. The Spirit of God is operative in the Church. Never before as in recent years has the teaching of the Catholic Church been so extensively reformulated, precisely with the issues that trouble the modern conscience in mind. It is sufficient to list the topics on which the Popes, the Ecumenical Council, the Synod of Bishops, and the various national episco-

pal conferences, including that of the Scottish bishops, have given authoritative and clear statements of Catholic belief and practice for the guidance of the faithful in these perplexing times. In the name of all the shepherds of Christ's flock, to whom the office of pastors and teachers has been divinely entrusted (Eph. 4:11), I assure you that we are acutely aware of the problems you have to face in life, and of the anxiety which so often fills your hearts.

MY LIFE'S WORK

12. In fulfilling that solemn charge of leading the flock to eternal life, we must keep ever in mind the words of the Apostle Paul to Timothy: "Proclaim the message and, welcome or unwelcome, insist on it. Refute falsehood, correct error, call to obedience—but do all with patience and with the intention of teaching.... Make the preaching of the Good News your life's work" (2 Tm. 4:2, 5).

Dear brothers and sisters! Preaching the Good News of Jesus is my life's work. In addition, I now have another ministry to fulfill in the Church, as Successor of Simon Peter, to whom Jesus Himself said: "I have prayed for you, Simon, that your faith may not fail.... You in your turn must strengthen your brothers" (Lk. 22:31). It is for this that I have come from Rome to Scotland. For this I joyfully accepted the invitation of your bishops to come and confirm you in our Catholic Faith "that comes to us from the apostles" (Roman Canon).

13. Allow me, therefore, to make my own the exhortation of St. Paul, addressed to you in today's liturgy: "I implore you to lead a life worthy of your

vocation" (Eph 4:1). And in Christ's own words, "You are the salt of the earth.... You are the light of the world" (Mt. 5:13-14), called by God our Father to be His apostles, prophets, evangelists, pastors and teachers to the men and women of this present generation, whom you must lead to Jesus, just as Andrew once led his brother Simon Peter. Your commitment to the sure ways of Christian living could well be decisive in bringing salvation to many. The world still recognizes genuine goodness for what it is!

A WORTHY LIFE

Be loyal to the memory of those valiant forerunners in the Faith. Be diligent in handing on intact the spiritual heritage committed to you. Be faithful to your daily prayers, to the holy Mass and the Sacrament of Penance, meeting regularly with Jesus as a loving and merciful Savior. Defend the sacredness of life and the holiness of matrimony. Understand your holy Catholic Faith and live by its teaching. Face up to the difficult challenges of modern life with Christian fortitude and patience. Did not Jesus Himself say to His disciples: "If anyone wants to be a follower of mine, let him renounce himself and take up his cross and follow me" (Mt. 16:24; Mk. 8:34)?

14. Beloved sons and daughters! I have been kept fully informed of the careful preparations, spread over many months, which have preceded my pastoral visit to Scotland. With admiration and satisfaction I have followed the intense program proposed by the bishops for a spiritual renewal of the Catholic community, to ensure that the effects of my visit produce fruits that will endure. From the depths of my heart I

thank each and every one of you for the prayers that have accompanied this preparation, for every effort that has been made to guarantee its success. "This is the day made memorable by the Lord: what immense joy for us!" (Ps. 118:24) I commend you all, bishops, clergy, religious and laity, to the maternal intercession of Mary, the Immaculate Mother of God and Mother of the Church.

15. Before concluding, I wish to address for a few moments that larger community of believers in Christ, who share with my Catholic brothers and sisters the privilege of being Scots, sons and daughters alike of this ancient nation. I know of the veneration in which you hold the Sacred Scriptures, accepting them for what they are, the Word of God, and not of man. I have reserved until now and should like to read to you the remaining words from that passage of St. Paul's letter to the Ephesians: "There is one body, one Spirit, just as you were all called. There is one Lord, one Faith, one baptism, and one God who is Father of all, over all, through all and within all" (Eph. 4:5-6). This passage clearly reveals the will of God for mankind, a plan human wills may oppose but cannot thwart. It is God's plan for all of us, "for there is no eternal city for us in this life but we look for one in the life to come" (Heb. 13:15). We are only pilgrims on this earth, making our way towards that heavenly kingdom promised to us as God's children. Beloved brethren in Christ, for the future, can we not make that pilgrimage together hand-in-hand, "bearing with one another charitably, in complete selflessness, gentleness and patience," doing all we can "to preserve the unity of the Spirit by the peace that binds us

together" (Eph. 4:2-3)? This would surely bring down upon us the blessing of God our Father on our pilgrim way.

As we now proceed to celebrate Christ's Eucharistic Sacrifice, let us remember all those—on both sides—who are affected by the conflict in the South Atlantic. In the joy of our celebration today we cannot permit ourselves to forget the victims of war, both the dead men and the wounded, as well as the broken hearts of many families.

Let us beseech the God of mercy to give us peace in this our day—the peace of Christ our Lord. Amen.

16. Beloved people of Scotland, in conclusion, I wish you and all who are dear to you, wherever they may be, the abundance of God's blessings, so that your families may prosper and peace and harmony may reign in your homes. May the prayers of the blessed Apostles Peter and Andrew obtain this for you!

And for your dearly beloved Scottish homeland I wish to adapt and make my own the words familiar to many of you: "Lord, let Scotland flourish through the preaching of Your Word and the praising of Your name!" Amen.

Fidelity and Friendship with Christ

In the Archbishop's residence in Edinburgh the Pope met the bishops of Scotland on the evening of June 1, and addressed them as follows.

Dear brothers in the Episcopate,

1. We have assembled this evening in the name of Jesus Christ, who is "the Shepherd and Bishop" of our souls (1 Pt. 2:25), "the chief Shepherd" of the flock (1 Pt. 5:14).

We are here to reflect on our episcopal ministry and to offer it to the Father through Christ our Lord, in whose name we exercise it. There are certainly many factors that affect our ministry and call for our response as leaders of God's people. And we have so many of these factors very much before our eyes at this time, when preoccupation for peace and reconciliation is so paramount in our minds. On such an occasion as this we perceive many obligations incumbent on us, precisely because we have been charged with "the ministry of reconciliation" (2 Cor. 5:18), precisely because we are called to preach a Gospel of peace.

2. But basic to the whole identity of a bishop is the fact that he is meant to be the living sign of Jesus Christ. "In the bishops," states the Second Vatican Council, "our Lord Jesus Christ, the supreme High Priest is present in the midst of those who believe" (LG 21).

3. This basic truth gives us a deep insight into ourselves and our need for holiness of life. The supernatural effectiveness of our ministry is linked in so many ways to our degree of holiness—to the degree in which we are configured to Christ by charity and grace. For this reason we should accept St. Paul's invitation as being directed mainly to ourselves: "Put on the new nature, created after the likeness of God in true righteousness and holiness" (Eph. 4:24).

Like Jesus we are called to preach conversion, to echo the words that He proclaimed so early in His public ministry: "Repent, and believe in the Gospel" (Mk. 1:14). But here too our effectiveness depends on our openness to grace; we ourselves are meant to experience the conversion that we proclaim. Holiness therefore becomes for us, as I mentioned to another group of bishops on another occasion, "the first priority in our lives and in our ministry" *(AAS:* 71 [1979], p. 1220).

4. There is no doubt about it: our fidelity to the love of Jesus and our friendship with Him are essential for all the apostolic works that are part of our daily lives. This fidelity to love, this friendship with the Christ whose kingdom we proclaim, must be nourished by our own prayer life. Only union with Christ makes it possible for us to be effective ministers of the Gospel. Let us remember the words of Jesus: "He who abides in me, and I in him, he it is that bears much fruit" (Jn. 15:5).

5. As bishops we are asked to meditate on the holiness of Christ. Indeed our people ask us for more than this: they want, and they need, the witness of a prophetic anticipation of the holiness to which we

invite them. They ask us to be their leaders in holiness, to trace out clearly for them the path for following Christ.

And so we must be, in the expression of St. Peter, "examples to the flock" (1 Pt. 5:3)—in leading the way in saying *yes* to God, *yes* to others, *yes* to the highest ideals of Christian life.

6. While the challenge is great, so also is the power of Christ's grace. Through adoration of the Eucharist you will find light and strength, gladness of heart, inspiration and the greatest means of holiness. And as the chief priest leading your people assembled for worship in the Eucharistic Sacrifice, you will find the fulfillment of your episcopal ministry.

In your own use of the Sacrament of Penance you will find renewed contact with the Christ whose compassionate representatives you are and who calls you personally to ever renewed conversion and holiness of life. You will find the means to give new assurance to your priests and people of the extreme relevance of this sacrament in the Church today. From your whole way of life—a life of union with God through prayer and penance—you will be still more zealous preachers of the mystery of salvation and eternal life: *Ex abundantia enim cordis os eius loquitur* (Lk. 6:45).

7. Indeed, everything in your lives, the whole apostolate of Scotland, will be seen from the vantage point of companionship with the Christ who has chosen you to preach His "unsearchable riches" (Eph. 3:8), to plead for peace, and to give your lives as He did, for the flock.

Dear brother bishops, in this collegial meeting this evening we have the wonderful opportunity to rededicate ourselves, together, to our episcopal ministry at the service of Christ and His Church. And in the vision that we have of this ministry we must always remember that Jesus Christ has first place in our lives. It was Christ who appointed the Twelve: "to be with him and to be sent out..." (Mk. 3:14).

8. This is our calling too, for ever: to be with Christ and by Him to be sent out—together—to proclaim the Good News of the kingdom of God. Through your holiness, and the holiness of the local Churches over which you preside and which you serve, may this Good News continue to spread throughout Scotland, for the glory of the most Holy Trinity—Father, Son and Holy Spirit.

May Mary, Queen of Peace and Mother of the Church, intercede for you and for all those who through your word will believe in the name of her Son, Jesus Christ.

Christ Is the True Bread Giving Life to the World

In Cardiff, the principal city of Wales, the Pope celebrated Mass in Pontcanna Fields, during which thirty children received their First Holy Communion. The text of his homily follows.

Dear friends in Christ,

1. Today the Bishop of Rome greets the people of Wales for the first time in their own beautiful land. It is a great joy for me to be with you here in Cardiff. I thank God for the privilege of celebrating the Eucharist with you, uniting with you in giving glory and praise to the Father and to the Son and to the Holy Spirit.

Gathered at this Mass are representatives from every Catholic parish in Wales and members of the Church who have come from England. I also greet those representing the other Christian communities of Wales. In the love of Christ I greet you all.

The people of Wales have an ancient tradition of allegiance to Christ. From the earliest Christian times, you have proclaimed your love of Christ, and you have sought to express this love through service to others and fidelity to the Word of God. The seed of God's Word first came to you from Rome; once planted, it took root, flowered and bore fruit. It found expression in your literature and left its imprint on your history. And it has remained alive in the hearts of every generation from Roman times down to the present age. It is this same Gospel which I proclaim to you today—the

Gospel of our Savior Jesus Christ, who is the Lord of history and the Bread of Life for a world in need of salvation.

THE GIFT OF THE EUCHARIST

2. The readings of the Mass today invite us to reflect on the mystery of the Eucharist. This great mystery was foreshadowed in Old Testament times when God provided the Israelites with manna in the wilderness. In the first reading, we hear the words Moses spoke to the people: "Remember how the Lord your God led you for forty years in the wilderness.... He fed you with manna which neither you nor your fathers had known, to make you understand that man does not live on bread alone but that man lives on everything that comes from the mouth of the Lord" (Dt. 8:2-3). God taught the people that He alone was their Lord. He alone was the One who would lead them out of slavery. He alone was the One who would care for them amid the hardships and sorrows they would encounter on the way to the promised land. When they were hungry and thirsty, he gave them manna from heaven and water from the rock.

What was foreshadowed in Old Testament times has been fulfilled in Jesus Christ. He gave His followers food for the journey of faith when He entrusted to the Church the gift of the Eucharist. Jesus Himself is the new spiritual food, for the Eucharist is His body and blood made present under the appearances of bread and wine. He Himself says in the Gospel: "I am the bread of life. He who comes to me will never be hungry; he who believes in me will never thirst" (Jn. 6:35).

Here in Wales, the Eucharist has held a place of prominence in the Church from the earliest times. This is shown by the Christian symbols of the Eucharist which have been discovered in the archaeological excavations at the Roman fort of Caerleon. Happily this great heritage has continued from the early beginnings down to the present time. This fact should not surprise us, since the Eucharist holds such a central place in Christian life and since the mystery of the Eucharist is so closely linked to the mystery of the Church. For every generation in the Church, the food which nourishes the People of God is the Eucharist, the body and blood of our Lord Jesus Christ.

OUR DAILY BREAD

3. What a beautiful prayer is recorded in today's Gospel. After Jesus speaks to the people about the true bread which comes down from heaven and gives life to the world, they cry out: "Give us that bread always" (Jn. 6:34). This prayer expresses a deep hunger on the part of the people, one which goes beyond the hunger for food. It is a hunger which arises from the depths of the soul and from the desire for love and fulfillment. It is a longing for wholeness and salvation and a yearning for fullness of life—it is a hunger for union with God. Christ is God's answer to this prayer, God's response to the deepest hunger of the human heart. All the anguished cries of mankind to God since the fall of Adam and Eve find fulfillment in the Son of God become man. Jesus still says: "I am the bread of life. He who comes to me will never be hungry; he who believes in me will never thirst" (Jn. 6:35). May this same prayer—"Give us that bread

always"—often be our prayer too. From our First Communion until the day we die, may we have a deep yearning for Christ, the true bread which gives life to the world.

4. And now I would like to speak to these little ones who are about to receive Holy Communion for the first time.

Dear children: Jesus is coming to you in a new way today, in a special way. He wants to live in you. He wants to speak to you in your heart. He wants to be with you all through your day.

Jesus comes to you in the Eucharist so that you will live forever. Holy Communion is not ordinary food. It is the bread of eternal life. It is something more precious than gold or silver. It is worth more than anything you can imagine. For this sacred bread is the body and blood of Jesus. And Jesus promises that if you eat His flesh and drink His blood, you will have life in you and you will live forever.

You come to the altar today with faith and prayer. Promise me that you will try to stay close to Jesus always, and never turn your back on Him. As you grow older, go on learning about Jesus by listening to His Word and by talking to Him in prayer. If you stay close to Him, you will always be happy.

GENUINELY CHRISTIAN

5. Dear parents of these children: your love for Christ has made this day possible. For you are your children's first teachers in the ways of faith. By what you say and do, you show them the truths of our Faith and the values of the Gospel. This is indeed not only a sacred duty, but a grace, a great privilege. Many other

members of the Church share in this task, but the main responsibility for your children's religious formation rests upon your shoulders. So try to make your homes genuinely Christian. Help your children to grow and mature as Jesus did at Nazareth, "in wisdom, in stature and in favor with God and men" (Lk. 2:52). Allow no one to take advantage of their lack of experience and knowledge. As you share with them in their personal pilgrimage to God, may you always be united in prayer and worship and in humble love of God and His people.

6. Dear teachers in our Catholic schools: you too deserve an honored place in our celebration today. Together with the parents, you help to prepare the children for the worthy reception of the sacraments and for a more active role in the Christian community. You bring them to a reverence and knowledge of God's Word and you explain to them the doctrine of the Church. And thus you introduce them gradually into the riches of the mystery of salvation.

You are heirs of a great tradition, and the People of God is in your debt. As you carry out your important mission in that special community of faith which is the Catholic school, may you have a deep love for the Church. May your love for the Church radiate through all your various activities and be reflected in the way you faithfully hand on the sacred deposit of the Faith.

HELP THEM GROW

7. Beloved brother priests: this is a day of joy for you also, for these little ones are members of the parishes in which you have the privilege to serve.

Together with their families and teachers, you introduce the children to the wider Christian community and help them to grow to the fullness of maturity in Christ. To them and to the whole parish, you seek to give a shepherd's care. May you be the best of shepherds and model your lives on our Lord and Redeemer.

I know that your bishops are anxious to develop throughout England and Wales practical programs of adult education in the Faith. I urge you to be in the vanguard of those efforts, which are so important for the vitality of the Church.

I also encourage you to make the worthy celebration of the Eucharist the first priority of your pastoral ministry. Recall the words of the Second Vatican Council: "The other sacraments, as well as every ministry of the Church and every work of the apostolate, are linked with the Holy Eucharist and are directed towards it. For the most blessed Eucharist contains the Church's entire spiritual wealth, that is, Christ Himself, our Passover and living bread" (PO 5). No other work you do is of greater importance for the Church or of greater service to your people. For the celebration of the Eucharistic Sacrifice is the source and summit of all Christian life. Ensure that the Mass is celebrated with deep reverence and prayerfulness, and make every effort to foster the active participation of the laity. Bear witness to the Church's faith in the Real Presence of Christ by your own daily visit of Eucharistic adoration (cf. *ibid.*, 18). And through the liturgical renewal that was willed by the Council, may all your parishes become communities alive with faith and charity.

8. My brothers and sisters in Christ, every time we gather for the Eucharist, we take part in the great mystery of faith. We receive the bread of life and the cup of eternal salvation. This is the cause of our joy and the source of our hope. As we speak of life and the Bread of Life, let us also remember those who have died in conflicts throughout the world: in the conflict in the South Atlantic, in the conflict between Iran and Iraq, in every place where human blood is shed. And in the power of the blood of Christ may we all find peace, reconciliation and eternal life. Amen.

Unity Is God's Gracious Gift

Before going to Ninian Park to meet the youth of England and Wales, Pope John Paul received in Cardiff Castle representatives of various Christian communities of Wales. During the meeting he addressed them as follows.

Dear brethren,

"Grace to you and peace from God the Father and the Lord Jesus Christ" (2 Thes. 1:2).

Since my visit to your city is brief, we are able to meet together for only a few moments, and you have very rightly proposed that these few moments should be devoted to a common prayer for unity. This is as it should be, for unity is God's gracious gift, and all our other efforts to do His will are vain if they are not rooted in change of heart, in holiness of life and in prayer for unity: these are the very soul of the ecumenical movement (cf. UR 8).

I have been happy to learn of the degree of cooperation that exists between Catholics and members of other Churches and communities in Wales, and of the part played by Catholic consultors and observers in the work of the Council of Churches in Wales. Last Saturday at Canterbury I was able to have a longer meeting with a group of British Church leaders, among them the representatives of the Churches of this country. Such meetings are important, for they bear witness to our desire to fulfill God's will for our unity with Him and with each other, in His Son, our Lord and Savior Jesus Christ. This witness is all the more needed in these troubled days in which the peace of the world is so sorely threatened. Let us then pray together, in the words our Savior gave us.

I Came to Great Britain To Invite You To Pray

At Ninian Park in Cardiff on the afternoon of June 2, the Holy Father met the youth of Wales and England and spoke to them as follows.

Dear young people, dear brothers and sisters in Jesus Christ,

As my visit to Britain draws to an end, I am happy that this last meeting is with you—the youth of England and Wales, you who are the hope of tomorrow.

I have come to this land as a pilgrim pastor, a servant of Jesus Christ. I have come to proclaim Christ's Gospel of peace and reconciliation; I have come to celebrate His saving action in the sacraments of the Church. I have come to call you to Christ.

1. Before I go away, there is something really important that I wish to emphasize. There is something very closely linked to the sacraments that I have celebrated, something that is essential to your Christian lives. *It is prayer.* Prayer is so important that Jesus Himself tells us: "Pray constantly" (Lk. 21:36). He wants us to pray for light and strength. He wants us to pray to His Father, as He Himself did. The Gospel tells us that Jesus prayed all night before choosing His Apostles (cf. Lk. 6:12). And later on, in His passion, at the height of His suffering, Christ "prayed more earnestly" (Lk. 22:44).

AS JESUS TAUGHT US

2. Jesus not only gave us the example of prayer, He actually taught us how to pray. One of the most beautiful scenes of the Gospel shows Jesus gathered

with His disciples, teaching them to pray: "Our Father who art in heaven, hallowed be thy name. Thy kingdom come, thy will be done, on earth as it is in heaven." Jesus was showing His disciples the value of praising God: the importance of God's name, His kingdom and His holy will. At the same time Jesus was telling them to ask for bread, for pardon and for help in trials. "Give us this day our daily bread; and forgive us our trespasses as we forgive those who trespass against us; and lead us not into temptation, but deliver us from evil" (cf. Mt. 6:9-13; Lk. 11:2-4).

THE PERSON OF JESUS

3. My dear young people, it is through prayer that Jesus leads us to His Father. It is in prayer that the Holy Spirit transforms our lives. It is in prayer that we come to know God: to detect His presence in our souls, to hear His voice speaking through our consciences, and to treasure His gift to us of personal responsibility for our lives and for our world.

It is through prayer that we can clearly focus our attention on the person of Jesus Christ and see the total relevance of His teaching for our lives. Jesus becomes the model for our actions, for our lives. We begin to see things His way.

4. Prayer transforms our individual lives and the life of the world. Young men and women, when you meet Christ in prayer, when you get to know His Gospel and reflect on it in relation to your hopes and your plans for the future, then everything is new. Everything is different when you begin to examine in prayer the circumstances of every day, according to

the set of values that Jesus taught. These values are so clearly stated in the beatitudes: "Blessed are the merciful, for they shall obtain mercy. Blessed are the pure of heart, for they shall see God. Blessed are the peacemakers, for they shall be called children of God" (Mt. 5:7-9).

In prayer, united with Jesus—your brother, your friend, your savior, your God—you begin to breathe a new atmosphere. You form new goals and new ideals. Yes, in Christ you begin to understand yourselves more fully. This is what the Second Vatican Council wanted to emphasize when it stated: "The truth is that only in the mystery of the Incarnate Word does the mystery of man take on light" (GS 22). In other words, Christ not only reveals God to man, but He reveals man to himself. In Christ we grasp the secret of our own humanity.

EXPERIENCING THE TRUTH

5. But there is more. Through prayer you come to experience the truth that Jesus taught: "The words that I have spoken to you are spirit and life" (Jn. 6:63). In Jesus, whom you get to know in prayer, your dreams for justice and your dreams for peace become more definite and look for practical applications. When you are in contact with the Prince of Peace, you understand how totally opposed to His message are violence and terrorism, hatred and war. In Him you experience the full meaning of an interpersonal relationship that is based on generous love. Christ offers you a friendship that does not disappoint, a fidelity beyond compare.

6. Through contact with Jesus in prayer, you gain a sense of mission that nothing can dull. Your Christian identity is reaffirmed, and the meaning of your lives is forever linked to Christ's saving mission. Through prayer, the commitments of your Baptism and Confirmation take on an urgency for you. You realize that you are called to spread Christ's message of salvation (cf. AA 3).

In union with Jesus, in prayer, you will discover more fully the needs of your brothers and sisters. You will appreciate more keenly the pain and suffering that burden the hearts of countless people. Through prayer, especially to Jesus at Communion, you will understand so many things about the world and its relationship to Him, and you will be in a position to read accurately what are referred to as the "signs of the times." Above all you will have something to offer those who come to you in need. Through prayer you will possess Christ and be able to communicate Him to others. And this is the greatest contribution you can make in your lives: *to communicate Christ to the world.*

STRENGTH THROUGH PRAYER

7. Through prayer you will receive the strength to resist the spirit of the world. You will receive the power to show compassion to every human being—just as Jesus did. Through prayer you will have a part in salvation history as it unfolds in your generation. In prayer you will be able to enter into the heart of Jesus and understand His feelings towards His Church. By using the Psalms—the prayerbook that Jesus used—you will be able to repeat, under the action of the Holy Spirit, the praise and thanksgiving that have

been offered to God for centuries by His people. In all the circumstances of your lives, you will find that Jesus is with you—He is close to you in prayer. It is prayer that will bring joy into your lives and help you to overcome the obstacles to Christian living. Remember the words of St. James: "Is any one among you suffering? Let him pray" (Jas. 5:13).

8. My dear young people, it is easy to see why Christ told us to pray all the time, and why St. Paul insisted on this so much (cf. Lk. 21:36; Rom. 12:12; 1 Thes. 5:7). It is in prayer that God finally brings us into union with Himself, through our Lord Jesus Christ, His Son, who lives and reigns with Him and the Holy Spirit for ever and ever.

When you go to Jesus in prayer—and through Him to the Father—you will always find inspiration in Mary His Mother. With every generation of disciples you will learn to pray with her, and with her to await the action of the Holy Spirit in your lives (cf. Acts 1:14).

9. It is my hope today, as I return to Rome, that you will remember why I came among you. And as long as the memory of this visit lasts, may it be recorded that I, John Paul II, came to Britain to call you to Christ, to invite you to pray!

Dear young people, this explains why, in the Church of today, you are the hope of tomorrow. And so I urge you, in the words of St. Paul: "Pray at all times in the Spirit...and also for me, that utterance may be given me in opening my mouth boldly to proclaim the mystery of the Gospel...that I may declare it boldly, as I ought to speak.... Grace be with all who love our Lord Jesus Christ with unfailing love" (Eph. 6:18-20, 24). Amen.

Great Blessing of Mutual Understanding and Respect

During a brief farewell ceremony before leaving Wales, the Holy Father, responding to the address of the Archbishop of Westminster, spoke as follows.

Dear friends,

1. My pastoral visit to the countries of Britain has now come to an end. I came here as a herald of peace, to proclaim a Gospel of peace and a message of reconciliation and love. I came also as a servant—the servant of Jesus Christ, my Savior; and the servant, too, of the Christian people. As I have traveled round England, Scotland, and finally Wales, in fulfillment of my pastoral duty to confirm my brethren, I have sought to remind Catholics of the whole saving activity of Christ, the Redeemer, our risen Lord. In each of the countries I have also been able to meet and to pray with our brethren from other Christian communities. For these wonderful opportunities and for the friendship and brotherly welcome I have received everywhere, I give praise to God and I thank you all.

2. To the civic authorities of the countries and of the cities I have visited, I wish to express my deep gratitude. The help, support and cooperation you have given to the Catholic people in your areas, and the way you have made available suitable places for my pastoral visit, have reminded the world of the great blessing of mutual understanding and respect

which are a part of the British inheritance. I also wish to thank the police and all those who have been responsible for public order and for the smooth running of the events of these past few days.

3. And now, as I prepare to return to Rome, I express once more my good wishes to all the people of Britain, and in particular to Her Majesty the Queen, especially on this the anniversary of her coronation. As I leave you, I do so with the prayer that God may bless all the people of these countries. To the people of Wales, among whom I have spent this memorable day, I say: *Bentith Duw Arnoch!*

To all the people of England, Scotland and Wales, I say: May God bless you all. May He make you instruments of His peace, and may the peace of Christ reign in your hearts and in your homes.

All Peoples Are United in the Body of Christ

On Wednesday, June 9, the Holy Father shared his reflections on his recent pastoral journey to Great Britain, addressing the following message to the crowds in St. Peter's Square.

1. When it was granted me to celebrate the Eucharistic Sacrifice in Westminster Cathedral in London with the Episcopate of England, Scotland and Wales, I thanked Christ for this sign of unity that embraces all men: the sign in which peoples, even if they are divided by temporary conflicts, do not cease being united in the mystery of the Body of Christ. Christ "in fact is our peace" (Eph. 2:14), to whom we must always reach out in our thoughts, our hearts and our deeds, so that the "spirit of the world" (1 Cor. 2:12), which pushes toward divisions and wars, will not rule mankind.

2. The papal journey to Great Britain had been prepared for a long time: it had been arranged two years previously, and for eight months had been carefully elaborated in the individual dioceses and parishes of England, Scotland and Wales. Today, speaking from the perspective of the now completed visit, I cannot but emphasize especially the dimensions of this preparation and its high level. It is a matter here not only of material means, but above all of the spiritual dimension of this great common labor. There was manifested in it something more than today's maturity of the People of God. There was manifested

the heritage of many centuries, which had its historical beginning in England in the person of St. Augustine, the first Bishop of Canterbury. In Scotland that beginning is linked with the names of Saints Ninian, Columba and Kentigern, and in Wales with St. David.

That heritage has behind it not only far-off beginnings (which for the rest bring us back even further than the names mentioned, right to the time of Imperial Rome)—but also a series of difficult centuries marked by the blood of modern martyrs, of whom we speak with veneration, but also without any human bitterness, as of the martyrs of the first centuries. We speak of them with a love worthy of that love to which they themselves, to quote St. John Fisher and St. Thomas More, gave testimony. And finally, there is in the last century the heritage linked to the name of the great Cardinal Newman: the heritage of the laborious search for truth as the way of unity in the Faith. Christianity in Great Britain is an important ecumenical ground. The Catholic Church is found in this land, accepting as its own the way of Christian unity, as the Second Vatican Council has pointed out.

3. About the visit itself, one can say that it was a pilgrimage through the seven holy sacraments, in which the life of the People of God is formed and developed. This theological and likewise pastoral form linked the whole geography of the visit with a uniform theme, beginning with Westminster Cathedral, where the theme was Baptism. The next day (the vigil of Pentecost) in Wembly Stadium, in front of the statue of Our Lady of Walsingham, the renewal of the baptismal promises was made. We were united in this prayer with the Mother of the Church, just like

the Apostles in the Upper Room when they were waiting for the coming of the Spirit Counselor. The same day, in the morning, in Canterbury Cathedral, all the participants in the meeting, Anglicans and Catholics, renewed their baptismal vows.

Still on the first day of the pilgrimage, the solemn and deeply penetrating liturgy of the Anointing of the Sick took place in the cathedral of Southwark—a great meeting with the Church of the suffering united with Christ.

4. The Eucharist celebrated on Pentecost itself, in a large field near Coventry, made present the coming of the Paraclete upon the place that particularly suffered destruction during the Second World War. The symbol of this destruction is the ancient cathedral, next to which a new one has been built. The Sacrament of Confirmation, administered during the Mass, illustrated the building up of the Church through faith and the works springing from it in the community of the People of God.

The same day of Pentecost, in the afternoon, I was in Liverpool, the largest center of Catholics in Great Britain. There was a greeting at the airport, in the presence of the magnificent crowd along the city's streets, who attended the visit first to the Anglican cathedral and then to the recently constructed Catholic cathedral. The theme during the Mass was the Sacrament of Penance and Reconciliation, in keeping with the words of the liturgy: "Whose sins you shall forgive, they are forgiven" (Jn. 20:2), and also in keeping with the great effort that Catholic and Anglican Christians make in this city in the direction of mutual reconciliation according to the spirit of the Gospel.

5. On Monday, the theme was primarily the Sacrament of Orders, highlighted through the conferral of priestly ordination during the solemn Eucharist in Manchester.

Then there was the Sacrament of Matrimony during the meeting with the representatives of families in a large field near York. In connection with the Liturgy of the Word and the homily, the couples and the members of the families renewed the promises that make up the basis of their community in Christ and in the Church.

In this context, I must add everything which during my pilgrimage referred to the Christian vocation in general, particularly to the priestly and religious vocation, through meetings with priests, brothers and sisters of orders and religious congregations, with the students of seminaries and novitiates: meetings, word, prayer.

6. The Eucharist was, in a certain sense, a continuous theme, at the center of every meeting. However, in a special and detailed way, it was emphasized in Cardiff, the last stop on the journey, where the First Communion of young Christians took place.

Youth had their special place in this pilgrimage. A special testimony of their presence in the Church was given twice: the first time, on the occasion of the meeting in Edinburgh (also with the youngest). The second, at the end of the whole program of the visit, in Cardiff. These meetings were full of a youthful spontaneity, and at the same time full of a profound Christian content. The last word addressed to the

Church in Great Britain was on the theme of prayer—and that was to the young people in Cardiff.

7. The visit in Scotland had its two poles in Edinburgh and Glasgow. They allowed the Church, that in Scottish land has a special history and a profile of its own, to gather and be seen. That was illustrated in both cities, but the main liturgical meeting was held in Glasgow on Tuesday afternoon, with an enormous participation of the faithful. The theme of the homily was a synthesis: the kingdom of God in its history and present realization on Scottish soil and in the history of the Scottish men and women.

Among others, I also had the opportunity to visit the educational community in Glasgow; and then there was the unforgettable visit to the community of the sick in Edinburgh.

8. The Church, which is the sacrament of the union of man with God and the sign of the unity of the whole human family, is found in the British Isles, as I have already said, in a particularly ecumenical ground. This was manifested in all the stops of the visit. First of all in England, with the historic meeting in Canterbury Cathedral, which is the See of the President of the entire Anglican Communion.

One can say that the preparation for this meeting was particularly long and laborious: twelve years of work by the Anglican and Catholic International Commission, which finally presented to the Pope and to the President of the Anglican Communion the results of its studies. These results have become a basis for the Common Declaration signed on the vigil of Pentecost. It constitutes a foundation for further ecumenical collaboration, which has as its aim paving the way to full unity.

It would be difficult to say something more in this concise description. We need only thank the Spirit of unity and truth, who guided our steps to this meeting and, we hope, will continue to guide them.

From the ecumenical viewpoint, the meeting with the representatives of the British Council of Churches in Canterbury, and then in Edinburgh another meeting with the representatives of the Christian communities of Scotland, also were important.

Moreover, special importance must be given, too, to the meeting with the Moderator of the General Assembly of the Church of Scotland (Presbyterian) in the same city of Edinburgh, which points out the special nature of the ecumenical way proper to Scotland.

9. On the occasion of this visit which was, above all, of a pastoral nature, I felt honored by the meeting with Queen Elizabeth II on the first day of my journey.

The representatives of the political authorities—given the international situation arising from the relations with Argentina—on their part expressed the initiative to withdraw from the program of the visit.

Realizing how much depended, in such an excellent preparation of the pilgrimage through England, Scotland and Wales, on different factors and on the important part played by the authorities, I wish to express once again my heartfelt gratitude to all.

10. The first visit in history made by the Bishop of Rome to Great Britain has certainly its unique historic eloquence. May I be granted to place it in the Heart of Him who is the Lord of history, the King of peace and the Prince of the world to come.

INDEX

Andrew, St. 114f., 146
Anglican-Roman Catholic International Commission 70
Anglicans 71
Anointing of the Sick 29f.
Augustine, St. 49, 53

Baptism 22f., 54
beatitudes 172
Bishop of Rome 21, 38; see also *Successor of Peter* and *Vicar of Christ*
bishop(s) 36ff., 65, 158ff.
Boniface, St. 77

Catholics 71
  of Argentina 12
  of Scotland 150f.
celibacy 44
Challoner, Bishop Richard 25f.
charisms 127
chastity 44
children 111, 166
Christ see *Jesus Christ*
Christian(s) 48, 50, 119
Christianity 116
Church 16, 19, 52f., 82, 86f., 95, 105, 181
  communion with 122f.
  in Scotland 150ff.
  local 36
College of Cardinals 35f.

collegiality 34ff.
  of the Catholic Episcopate 39
Common Declaration 57
communion
  among Christians 59f.
communities
  contemplative 126
  religious 125
confidence
  in God 83
Confirmation 78
conflict
  in the South Atlantic 12, 15ff.
conscience
  Christian 153
consecration 102
contemplation 126
conversion 159
  interior 88
cooperation
  between Catholics and members of other Churches 169
cross 85f.
culture
  Polish 93ff.

dialogue
  between Catholic Church and other Churches 69ff., 130
dignity
  human 63
disunity 88
Divine Master 147

ecumenism 88
education 96, 137ff.
  Catholic 143
  involvement of parents in 140f.
  of the whole person 140
educators 143
emigration 92, 94f.
Eucharist 124, 160, 167f.
  mystery of the 163f.
evangelical counsels 43, 125
evangelization 18
evil 85f.

faith 20, 54, 146f.
Familiaris consortio 112
family 96f., 109, 113
  Christian 110
fidelity 159
formation
  religious 166
friendship
  between Poland and Britain 81

generosity
  of Britain 81
God 64ff., 83, 87, 98, 100, 148f., 156, 163, 171
  union with 57, 164f.
Good News 123, 154, 161
Good Shepherd 72
Gospel 24, 66, 162, 171
  values of 66
grace 160
Gregory, Pope 72

handicapped 31, 132f.
history 93
  of Church in Scotland 149ff.
  of England 107f.
  of Poland 94
holiness 159f.
Holy Communion 165
Holy Spirit 22, 54f., 67, 76, 79, 86, 88f., 116f.
hope 83

identity
  Christian 173
integrity
  of catechetical message 143

Jesus Christ 24, 29f., 42, 46, 52, 75, 85ff., 94f., 112, 115f., 124, 133, 143, 145ff., 149, 159ff., 163ff., 170ff., 177
  confidence in 119f.
  death of 22
  person of 171
  Shepherd 26
John Fisher, St. 25
John Ogilvie, St. 151

knowledge 144f.

laity 37, 124
life
  Christian 49, 66, 147
  consecrated 43
  dignity of 132
  right to 30f.
  ultimate meaning of 145
love 111, 148
  commandment of 57f.
  of husband and wife 109
  of Jesus Christ 30

Magisterium 127
man 63, 96
Margaret Sinclair, Venerable 134f.
marriage 108f.
  between Catholics and other baptized Christians 109
  indissolubility of 112
martyrs 50, 103
Mary 64ff., 98, 127f., 174
  Blessed Lady 120
  Mother of Jasna Gora 97
  Our Lady of Czestochowa 98
Mass 65, 167
mercy
  of God 85
ministry 154
  episcopal 158
  of priests 123
  of reconciliation 158
  of the priesthood 65
missionaries 80
monasticism 40

INDEX

Newman, Cardinal John Henry 77

obedience 44
ordination 104, 106

parent(s) 111, 165f.
  as primary educators 140f.
Paul, St. 118, 123
Paul VI, Pope 70
peace 15, 38, 75
penance 84, 102f.
Penance
  Sacrament of 87, 160
Pentecost 22f., 78
People of God 23
perseverance 43
Peter, St. 21
Poland 91ff.
poverty 44
prayer 64f., 71, 103, 159, 170ff.
  strength through 173
priest(s) 36, 103, 121ff., 166f.
  in the work of reconciliation 87
priesthood 65, 102, 105, 122
prisoners 104
promises
  baptismal 64

Ramsey, Archbishop Michael 70
reconciliation 19, 38, 59, 84ff.
relationship
  with Jesus Christ 172
religious 36f., 41ff., 121ff.
religious life 41, 105
  contemplative 44; see also
    communities
renewal
  spiritual 101
rosary 64

sacrament(s) 178f.
saints 25
St. Andrew's College 136
schools
  Catholic 141f.
Scotland 149
Second Vatican Council 41, 88, 167; see also *Vatican Council II*

Sermon on the Mount 147
service
  ecclesial 126
sick 31
sin(s)
  forgiveness of 86
  remission of 85
Successor of Peter 11, 154; see also *Bishop of Rome* and *Vicar of Christ*
suffering(s) 82
  value of 28ff.

teachers 142f., 166
teaching
  of the Church 153
The Catholic School 142
Thomas More, St. 25
truth 95, 172

unemployment 82
union
  with God 174
unity 16, 20f., 23, 50, 52ff., 57, 69, 71, 88, 130f., 156, 169, 177, 181
  Christian 18, 24, 60f.
university(ies)
  purpose of 144f.

values
  moral 31, 66f., 93, 145
  spiritual 93, 145
Vatican Council II 36f.; see also *Second Vatican Council*
Vicar of Christ 34; see also *Bishop of Rome* and *Successor of Peter*
virginity 44
vocation 149
  Christian 67f.

war 27, 74
weakness 31
witness 11
work 116
world
  spirit of the 153
Wyszynski, Cardinal Stefan 97

young people 75f., 78, 83, 114, 124, 170, 174, 180

Daughters of St. Paul

IN MASSACHUSETTS
50 St. Paul's Ave., Jamaica Plain, Boston, MA 02130;
617-522-8911.
172 Tremont Street, Boston, MA 02111; **617-426-5464;**
617-426-4230.

IN NEW YORK
78 Fort Place, Staten Island, NY 10301; **212-447-5071; 212-447-5086.**
59 East 43rd Street, New York, NY 10017; **212-986-7580.**
625 East 187th Street, Bronx, NY 10458; **212-584-0440.**
525 Main Street, Buffalo, NY 14203; **716-847-6044.**

IN NEW JERSEY
Hudson Mall — Route 440 and Communipaw Ave.,
Jersey City, NJ 07304; **201-433-7740.**

IN CONNECTICUT
202 Fairfield Ave., Bridgeport, CT 06604; **203-335-9913.**

IN OHIO
2105 Ontario Street (at Prospect Ave.), Cleveland, OH 44115;
216-621-9427.
25 E. Eighth Street, Cincinnati, OH 45202; **513-721-4838;**
513-421-5733.

IN PENNSYLVANIA
1719 Chestnut Street, Philadelphia, PA 19103; **215-568-2638.**

IN VIRGINIA
1025 King Street, Alexandria, VA 22314; **703-683-1741;**
703-549-3806.

IN FLORIDA
2700 Biscayne Blvd., Miami, FL 33137; **305-573-1618.**

IN LOUISIANA
4403 Veterans Memorial Blvd., Metairie, LA 70002; **504-887-7631;**
504-887-0113.
1800 South Acadian Thruway, P.O. Box 2028, Baton Rouge, LA 70821;
504-343-4057; 504-381-9485.

IN MISSOURI
1001 Pine Street (at North 10th), St. Louis, MO 63101; **314-621-0346;**
314-231-1034.

IN ILLINOIS
172 North Michigan Ave., Chicago, IL 60601; **312-346-4228;**
312-346-3240.

IN TEXAS
114 Main Plaza, San Antonio, TX 78205; **512-224-8101; 512-224-0938**

IN CALIFORNIA
1570 Fifth Ave., San Diego, CA 92101; **619-232-1442.**
46 Geary Street, San Francisco, CA 94108; **415-781-5180.**

IN WASHINGTON
2301 Second Ave., Seattle, WA 98121.

IN HAWAII
1143 Bishop Street, Honolulu, HI 96813; **808-521-2731.**

IN ALASKA
750 West 5th Ave., Anchorage, AK 99501; **907-272-8183.**

IN CANADA
3022 Dufferin Street, Toronto 395, Ontario, Canada.

IN ENGLAND
128, Notting Hill Gate, London W11 3QG, England.
133 Corporation Street, Birmingham B4 6PH, England.
5A-7 Royal Exchange Square, Glasgow G1 3AH, England.
82 Bold Street, Liverpool L1 4HR, England.

IN AUSTRALIA
58 Abbotsford Rd., Homebush, N.S.W. 2140, Australia